Unusual Stories from Many Lands

ARLO T. JANSSEN
Cochise Community College

Illustrations by Rosa Lopez

 Prentice Hall Regents, Englewood Cliffs, NJ 07632

Library of Congress Cataloging in Publication Data

Janssen, Arlo T. (date)
    Unusual stories from many lands.

    1. English language—Text-books for foreign
speakers. 2. College readers. 3. Short stories.
I. Lopez, Rosa. II. Title.
PE1128.J34 1985   428.6'4   84–11674
ISBN 0-13-937707-7

Editorial/production supervision and
        interior design: Barbara Alexander
Cover design: George Cornell
Manufacturing buyer: Harry P. Baisley

©1985 by Prentice Hall Regents
Prentice-Hall, Inc.
A Simon & Schuster Company
Englewood Cliffs, New Jersey 07632

Printed in the United States of America
20   19   18   17   16

ISBN 0-13-937707-7

90000

9 780139 377075

Prentice-Hall International (UK) Limited, *London*
Prentice-Hall of Australia Pty. Limited, *Sydney*
Prentice-Hall Canada Inc., *Toronto*
Prentice-Hall Hispanoamericana, S. A., *Mexico*
Prentice-Hall of India Private Limited, *New Delhi*
Prentice-Hall of Japan, Inc., *Tokyo*
Simon & Schuster Asia Pte. Ltd., *Singapore*
Editora Prentice-Hall do Brasil, Ltda., *Rio de Janeiro*

To OFELIA, the joy of my life

Contents

Preface   xi

The Recurring Dream   2

A ghost story told by a student from England, approximately 775 words in length. Both the story and the exercises use the simple *present tense* only. (Even the present *progressive* is avoided.) Exercises: A. Questions on content. B. Vocabulary practice (choosing correct meaning, verb matching and adjective matching).   C. Grammar practice (present tense of verbs). D. Questions for discussion. E. More items for speaking practice. F. Writing practice G. Reading practice. H. A bit of humor.

The Lost Doll   10

A story based on an incident told by a student from Colombia, South America, approximately 1,150 words in length. The story uses the *present* and the *past tenses*, but avoids the progressive forms. Exercises: A. Questions on content. B. Vocabulary practice (choosing correct meaning, adjective matching, verb matching. C. Grammar practice. D. Items for discussion. E. Story telling. F. Writing practice. G. A bit of humor.

The House Call   20

A ghost story told by a student from West Germany, approximately 900 words in length. Both the story and exercises use the *present* and *past progressive*, in addition to the simple present and past tense verb forms. Exercises: A. Questions on content. B. Vocabulary practice (choosing correct meaning). C. Grammar practice (changing simple, present verb form to past). D. More grammar practice (changing simple present and past tense verb forms to the progressive). E. Questions for discussion. F. Story telling. G. Writing practice. H. Reading practice. I. A bit of humor.

Meet Death   30

A story based on the "Pardoner's Tale" in the *Canterbury Tales* by Goeffrey Chaucer, approximately 1300 words in length. The *future tense* is used with *will, going to, the progressive with future meaning,* and *shall.* Exercises: A. Questions on content. B. Vocabulary practice (choosing the correct meaning, verb matching, and practice with *whose* and *who's*). C. Grammar practice (practice with *will, going to, the progressive with future meaning* and *shall.*) D. Items for discussion. E. Story telling. F. Writing practice. G. Reading practice. H. A bit of humor.

Feast in the Desert   43

A story told by a student from Kuwait, approximately 1200 words in length, with special practice with *commands.* Exercises: A. Questions on content. B. Vocabulary practice (word meaning, verb matching, and adjective matching). C. Grammar practice (practice with command, object–subject pronouns, choosing verb forms). D. Questions for discussion. E. Writing practice. F. A bit of humor.

Snowstorm   56

A ghost story based on an incident which occurred near Tucson, Arizona, approximately 1500 words in length, which uses the *present perfect* verb tense. Exercises: A. Questions on content. B. Vocabulary practice (choosing the correct meaning, practice with *no* and *any,* and adjective matching). C. Grammar practice (choosing correct verb tense). D. Items for discussion. E. Writing practice. F. A bit of humor.

The Hanging Tree   68

A ghost story based on an incident reported by a student from Sudan, Africa, approximately 1200 words in length, which uses the *past perfect* verb tense. Exercises: A. Questions on content. B. Vocabulary practice (choosing the correct meaning, verb matching, adjective matching, and practice with two uses of the verb *hang.*) C. Items for discussions or writing practice. D. A bit of humor.

Going Fishing   78

A story based on an incident reported by a student from Qatar, approximately 1200 words in length, with more practice with the *present* and *past perfect* tenses. Exercises: A. Questions on content, B. Vocabulary practice (choosing the correct meaning, adjective matching, and adverb matching). C. Grammar practice (choosing correct verb form). D. Writing practice (sentence completion). E. Items for discussion. F. Story telling. G. A bit of humor.

In the Operating Room   88

A story based on an incident reported by two Canadian citizens, approximately 1150 words in length. No new grammatical forms. Exercises: A. Questions on content. B. Vocabulary practice (choosing the correct meaning, verb matching and adjective matching). C. Items for discussion or writing practice. D. A bit of humor.

Patrick Hannigan   96

A story told by a student from Ireland, approximately 875 words in length. Exercises: A. Questions on content. B. Vocabulary practice (word meaning, practice with *rear* and *raise*, work with prepositions, and adjective matching). C. Grammar practice (choosing forms of verbs). D. Items for discussion. E. Story telling. F. Writing practice. G. A bit of humor.

Fear   105

A story told by a student from Mexico, approximately 1400 words in length, with special practice with *comparison of adjectives*. Exercises: A. Questions on content. B. Vocabulary practice (word meaning and verb matching). C. Grammar practice (comparison of adjectives and verb practice). D. Items for discussion. E. Writing practice. F. A bit of humor.

The Little Christmas Visitor   117

A story based on an incident told by a student from France, approximately 1400 words in length, with special practice with the *passive* voice. Exercises: A. Questions on content. B. Vocabulary practice (word meaning and verb matching). C. Grammar practice (practice with the passive voice and choosing verb forms). D. Items for discussion. E. Writing practice. F. A bit of humor.

The Whirlpool   129

A story told by a student from Bangladesh, approximately 1250 words in length. Exercises: A. Questions on content. B. Vocabulary practice (word meaning and verb matching). C. Grammar practice (verb forms, prepositions into and onto, and practice with tag questions). D. Items for discussion. E. Writing practice.

Dennis O'Day and the Leprechaun   139

Based on a story from Ireland, approximately 1600 words in length. Exercises: A. A true or false quiz on the content. B. Vocabulary practice (word meaning, adjective matching, and matching of two-word verbs). C. Grammar practice (practice with adjectives, adverbs, subject and object pronouns). D. Items for discussion. E. Writing practice. F. A bit of humor.

Was It a Dream?   152

A story by Guy de Maupassant, adapted for ESL. Exercises: A. Questions on content. B. Vocabulary practice (word meaning and verb matching). C. Grammar practice (practice with verbs, adjectives and adverbs). D. Items for discussion. E. Writing practice. F. A bit of humor.

The Loving Mother   161

Based on the story told by a student from Japan, 1150 words. Exercises: A. Questions on content. B. Vocabulary practice (word meaning, verb matching, sentences with the past tense). C. Items for discussion. D. Writing practice. E. A bit of humor.

Life in Death 169

Based on the "Oval Portrait" by Edgar Allan Poe, adapted for ESL, 700 words. Exercises: A. True or false quiz on content. B. Vocabulary practice (word meaning, verb matching, and practice with prefix dis-). C. Grammar practice (practice with verb forms and sentences with verbs). D. Items for discussion. E. Writing practice. F. A bit of humor.

Unexpected Reunion 179

A story, approximately 1150 words in length, by Johann Peter Hebel, adapted for ESL. Exercises: A. True or false quiz on content. B. Vocabulary practice (word meaning, verb matching and homonyms). C. Grammar practice (writing verb forms). D. Items for discussion. E. Food for thought.

Marta 190

A story, approximately 1650 words in length, based on an incident told by a student from Norway. Exercises: A. True or false quiz on content. B. Vocabulary practice (word meaning and matching verbs). C. Grammar practice (prepositions *in, on* and *at* and choosing verb forms). D. Items for discussion. E. Writing practice. F. A bit of humor.

The Open Window 202

A story by Saki (H. H. Munro), approximately 1325 words in length, adapted for ESL. Exercises: A. True or false quiz on content. B. Vocabulary practice (word meaning and matching adjectives). C. Grammar practice (choosing verb forms and practice with adjectives and adverbs). D. Items for discussion. E. Writing practice. F. A bit of humor.

Irregular Verbs 211

Preface

Unusual Stories from Many Lands contains twenty stories, all unusual, all interesting, all short, and all designed to help the student learn to converse more effectively in the English language. Five of the twenty stories are English-as-a-second-language (ESL) adaptations of some unusual and fascinating stories told in a few words by masters of the art: Chaucer, Saki (H. H. Munro), Poe, de Maupassant, and Hebel. The other fifteen stories are my own creations, based on incidents, occurrences, or stories told by students I have taught and/or interviewed in my nearly twenty years of teaching and supervising ESL classes at Cochise College.*

Some are "ghost stories," yet none is of the "blood and guts" or "horror" type. All are, instead, interesting and often light-hearted stories based on unusual experiences or unexplainable phenomena from various cultures. I use this type of story because I have found that even the most timid ESL student is inclined to speak when something unusual or mysterious is being discussed. And getting students to express themselves is very important in language teaching, of course.

Regarding the unusual and mysterious, however, let me emphasize that *it is not my intention that anything about ghosts or spirits should be taught in the classes where this book is used.* After all, *ESL courses are designed to teach English.* Therefore, any course material, whether about unusual phenomena or everyday occurrences, should help the student learn the English language. In a *debate class*, by comparison, the purpose is not to solve the problems of the world but to use those problems to learn the techniques of argumentation. Likewise, *in an ESL class, the topics used for discussion are only vehicles for learning language.*

It is important, also, to remember that *all the stories in this book are fiction*, although some are based on experiences or occurrences reported as fact. It is my hope that they will interest your students as much as they have mine.

Adding to the interesting aspect of the unusual content is the fact that the stories come from many cultures. The fifteen stories based on material from students represent fourteen countries (named under the titles of the stories). The other five stories are also from four different countries.

---

*Cochise College, located on the border of Mexico at Douglas, Arizona, has students from many countries of the world because of its strong ESL program. At this writing, nearly 10 percent of the full-time students on the main campus are from countries other than the United States.

In addition to being interesting, the stories are short. In most cases they are short enough to be introduced and presented in one class period, with perhaps one more period for the lesson material. The longest story is little more than 1,700 words and the shortest only 700, the average being approximately 1,100 words.

The greatest advantage of the book is that the material progresses in difficulty from a lower-intermediate to an upper-intermediate or lower-advanced level. This progression in difficulty is in the general content, especially in the grammar and usage of the language.

The progression is the most evident in the use of verb forms. The first story, for example, is told in the simple *present tense* only. The second story uses the *past tense*, but *progressive forms* in both present and past are avoided until the third story. The *future* is not used until the fourth story, and the fifth story emphasizes *commands*. The *present perfect* is not used until story six, and the *past perfect* is used the first time in story seven. The *passive voice* is avoided until the eleventh story.

In addition, there are other grammatical items stressed in the lesson material, and vocabulary lessons are included with all stories. There is also storytelling and reading and writing practice as well as a bit of humor in the lesson material.

Vocabulary lists are not included at the beginning of the stories. However, for those who like to go over word meanings before beginning a story, a glance at the vocabulary practice in the lesson material will be helpful. A list of the irregular verbs used in the stories is at the back of the book.

Incidentally, it is my considered opinion that every ESL student should learn to use an *English* dictionary as soon as possible and should be discouraged from using any dictionary that attempts to *translate* word meanings.

I have had a delightful time collecting material for and preparing *Unusual Stories from Many Lands*, and it has been gratifying to see the positive reaction of my students with whom the materials were "tested." I am quite confident that it will be of benefit in all ESL courses at this level, and it should be especially helpful as a supplementary text—adding some fun as well as reinforcement to the often difficult task of learning a new language.

ARLO T. JANSSEN
Douglas, Arizona

The Recurring Dream

A story from England.

Kimberly Clark who lives and works in London, England, seems like a
normal young woman of twenty-five. She's pretty, she loves to dance,
and she has many friends. Also, she has a good position in the office of a
large company.

5   Kim Clark does have a problem, however. The problem is that she
has a mysterious dream. It's mysterious because it is a dream about a
person and a place which are completely strange to her. And it is mysterious also because it is a recurring dream. That is, she dreams the same
thing frequently. Finally, she has the same dream almost every night.

10   The strange dream always begins on a country road. Kim stands on
this road and sees a lane with a white fence and a hedge on each side. At
the end of the lane, on the top of a little hill, she sees a small, white
cottage with green shutters. In the dream, she then walks up the lane to
the house, goes in, and looks around. In one of the rooms she finds a

15   man asleep in bed. He is a little, old man with white hair and a white
beard. In the dream, when Kim comes near his bed, the man wakes up.
Then he sits up and looks at her. When Kim opens her mouth to speak
to him, however, she wakes up in her apartment in London.

    The dream bothers Kim very much. It's all so strange! She knows no

20   place or house like that. She doesn't know any little, old man like that
either. And yet, night after night she has the same dream. In the dream,
she's always on the same country road. She sees the same lane with the
same hedge and white fence. And at the end of the lane stands the same
small, white cottage with green shutters. And each time, when she

enters the house and looks around, she sees the same little, old man 25
asleep in bed. And every time, when she opens her mouth to speak to
him, she wakes up in her own bed in London.

Kimberly speaks frequently with her roommate, Janet Wilson, about
the recurring dream. One day Janet says, "Kim, let's go out to my
parents' farm for a few days. It's so peaceful there."   30

"That sounds like a good idea," answers Kim with tears in her eyes.
"The dream troubles me so much. It's on my mind constantly."

Kim and Janet make plans to go to the country. And early the next
Saturday morning they leave the city in Janet's car. As soon as they are
away from the sights and sounds of the city, Kim sits back on the seat   35
beside her friend and closes her eyes. A little later, as Janet turns the car
onto a country road, Kim wakes up. In a second, her eyes open wide.

"There it is, Jan!" she exclaims. "There it is!"

"There is what?"

"The place!"   40

"What place?"

"The place in my dream! Look!"

"Please, Kim, forget about your dream! You only imagine this place is
the same! There are many places like this in the country!"

"No, Jan, it's not my imagination! This is the place! There is the lane   45
with the hedge and white fence! And look! There is the little, white
cottage with green shutters! Please, Jan, let me out!"

Janet stops the car and turns to her friend. "Please don't go up there,
Kim! It's not a good idea! Let's go on!"

"No, Jan! Let me go! I have to go and see!"   50

Kimberly opens the door of the car and gets out. First, she stands on
the road, just as she always does in the dream. Then she walks slowly up
the lane with the hedge and white fence on both sides. Her heart
pounds when she finally stands in front of the little, white cottage.
Everything looks exactly the same, except for a sign in front of the house 55
which says FOR SALE.

Kim goes to the door of the house and knocks. Her hands tremble as
she waits. In a minute the door opens. And there in the doorway stands
a little, old man with white hair and a white beard! The same as in her
dream! Her whole body shakes.   60

When the old man sees Kim, his eyes open wide, and he immediately
closes the door.

"Oh, don't close the door!" cries Kim. "Please! I have to talk to you!"

The man opens the door a little and looks at her. "What do you want
here?" he asks. "Why don't you go away?"   65

Kim doesn't know what to say. But she does want to talk to him. "I—I see—I see that this house is for sale," she stammers.

"Yes it is. But I'm sure *you* don't want to buy it!"

"Why do you say that?"

70 "Because—uh—because a ghost haunts this house."

"A ghost haunts this pretty, little house?"

"Yes, it comes almost every night now."

Kim tries hard to think of something to say. "Do—uh—do you know who the ghost is?" she stammers.

75 "Yes, I do now."

"Who is it?"

In a loud whisper he exclaims, "It's you!" Then he closes the door.

Note: This story uses only the simple *present tense*. Although I'm sure that you are able to use other English verb tenses quite well by now, it may be good for you to practice the use of the present tense. For this reason, all the exercises for this story use only the present tense.

A.   Questions on the *content* of the story.

(Can you answer with *only the present tense?*)

1. In which country does this story take place?
2. How old is Kim at this time?
3. Who is Kim's roommate?
4. Where is the house in Kimberly's dream?
5. Describe the lane and the house.
6. Describe the man Kim sees in the house.
7. Where, in the house, is the man when she sees him?
8. Where does Janet want to take Kim for a few days?
9. Where does Kim see a house like the one in her dream?
10. What does she do when she sees the house?
11. What does the little, old man do when he sees Kim at the door?

B.   Vocabulary practice.

1. Underline the correct answers.
   a. A *recurring* dream is one which happens (once in a while/ once/frequently).
   b. Kimberly says that she thinks about the dream *constantly,*

which means that she thinks about it (all the time/sometimes/once in a while).

   c. A *cottage* is a (little house/a house with shutters/a white house).

   d. A *mysterious* dream is a dream which is (recurring/strange/in the country).

   e. When Kim's roommate says, "You only *imagine* this place is the same," she means that Kim (thinks/knows/understands) that this place is the same.

   f. The *lane* in this story is (one side of a freeway/a pathway/an alley).

   g. Kim's heart *pounds* as she stands in front of the cottage because (she has a headache/she is nervous/she has heart trouble).

   h. A FOR SALE sign in front of a house indicates that the person who owns it wants to (sell it/rent it/buy it).

   i. Kim *stammers* when she tries to talk to the man because (she doesn't know what to say/she wants to buy the house/she sees a ghost).

   j. When the man says "A ghost *haunts* this house," he means that (a ghost comes to the house/a ghost wakes people up in the house/a ghost scares people in the house).

2. Match the words and phrases which have more or less the *same* meaning.

a. take place	1. enter
b. go in	2. trouble
c. find	3. discover
d. bother	4. shake
e. speak	5. talk
f. tremble	6. happen
g. close	7. haunt
	8. shut

3. Match the *opposites*.

a. same	1. different
b. strange	2. late
c. old	3. familiar
d. early	4. soft
e. white	5. good
f. hard	6. black
	7. young

C. Practice with present tense.

Choose the correct form of the verb.

1. Kimberly (work/works) for a large company.
2. Kim and her roommate (live/lives) in London.
3. The girl (look/looks) at the cottage on the hill.
4. The little house (have/has) green shutters.
5. The girls (go/goes) to the country.
6. Jan does not (dream/dreams) about a little, old man.
7. All people (have/has) dreams.
8. The man does not (sleep/sleeps) on the floor.
9. Kim (know/knows) no old man like this.
10. She doesn't (know/knows) this place either.
11. Cottages do not always (have/has) green shutters.
12. Ghosts sometimes (haunt/haunts) houses.
13. I (think/thinks) he wants to sell the house.
14. Do you sometimes (see/sees) strange things?
15. I think you and I sometimes (imagine/imagines) things.

D. Questions for *discussion*.

1. What do you think is the reason some people have recurring dreams?
2. Why do you think *Kim* has this dream?
3. It says in the story that Kim simply *goes into* the house in her dream, but it does not say *how* she enters. How do you think she enters? (Remember the ending of the story.)
4. In your opinion, why does Kim wake up each time she tries to speak to the man in her dream?
5. Why does Janet want to take Kim to her parents' farm for a few days?
6. When Kim sees a cottage like the one in her dream, Janet does *not* want her to go see it. Why?
7. Why does Kim's body shake when she sees the little, old man at the door of the cottage?
8. Why does the little, old man close the door when he sees Kim?
9. Why does Kim say something about the FOR SALE sign?
10. Why do you think the cottage is for sale?

E. More speaking practice.

(If the class is large, divide into smaller groups.)

1. Tell the story in your own words. One person can begin, another continue, and so on. (For practice, can you tell it in the present tense?)
2. Make up questions of your own about the story to ask others in the class. (If you ask "yes or no" questions, ask also "why?" or "why not?")

F.   More discussion (or writing practice).

1. Tell about an experience with a *strange dream* (a dream of yours or of someone you know).
2. Some people think *all* dreams have special meanings. What do you think? Tell about it, using examples, if you can.
3. Tell what you know about people in your part of the world who say that their bodies can be in one place while their "spirits" are in another. Explain.
4. Tell about a personal experience with a person who says his body can be in one place while the "spirit" is in another.

G.   Reading practice.

Practice reading one of these dialogues with another member of the group. Try to read it *with feeling*, the way you think they speak in the story.

1. A diaglogue between Kim and Jan.

> *Kim:* "There it is, Jan! There it is!"
> *Jan:* "There is what?"
> *Kim:* "The place!"
> *Jan:* "What place?"
> *Kim:* "The place in my dream! Look!"
> *Jan:* "Please, Kim forget about your dream! You only imagine this place is the same! There are many places like that in the country!"
> *Kim:* "No, Jan, it's not my imagination! This is the place! There is the lane with the hedge and white fence! And look! There is the little, white cottage with green shutters! Please, Jan, let me out!"
> *Jan:* "Please don't go up there, Kim! It's not a good idea! Let's go on!"
> *Kim:* "No, Jan! Let me go! I have to go and see!"

2. A dialogue between Kim and the little, old man.

Kim: "Oh, don't close the door! Please! I have to talk to you!"
Old Man: "What do you want here? Why don't you go away?"
Kim: "I—I see—I see that this house is for sale."
Old Man: "Yes, it is. But I'm sure *you* don't want to buy it!"
Kim: "Why do you say that?"
Old Man: "Because—uh—because a ghost haunts this house."
Kim: "A ghost haunts this pretty, little house?"
Old Man: "Yes. It comes almost every night now."
Kim: "Do—uh—do you know who the ghost is?"
Old Man: "Yes, I do now."
Kim: "Who is it?"
Old Man: "It's you!"

H.   A bit of humor.

Jim: You have to go to London on business sometimes, don't you, Harry?
Harry: Yes, I do, at least four times a year.
Jim: What do you think of London?
Harry: The city of London, to me, is like a cemetery.
Jim: A *cemetery?*
Harry: Yes. Like a cemetery, London is a nice place *to visit* but not a
   good place to make your permanent residence.

A friend of mine tells the story about a man who tries to train his dog.
Over and over he says to the dog, "Lay down! Lay down!" But, the dog
does not obey. Again he tries, and this time he *shouts* at the beautiful
animal, "Lay down! Lay down!" Again, nothing happens.
   A ten-year-old schoolboy who watches the man and his dog walks up to
the man and says, "That's an English setter, isn't it, Sir?"
   "Why, yes," replies the man. "Why do you ask?"
   "Well, if it's an *English* setter, Sir, I think you should say, *lie* down."

The Lost Doll

Based on a story told by Maria Wong of Colombia, South America.

Little Maria del Carmen was the only child of her parents, Roberto and Rosa Soto. "Carmen," as everyone called her, was a beautiful child. She was also bright, kind, and loving. However, the little girl was sick from the day of her birth. As time went on, her condition became worse. By
5 the time she turned four, she was very weak. A few days later, the frail child died.

After the funeral mass, Carmen's father, Roberto, put the small
Almost everyone in the village attended Carmen's funeral the next day. As they all passed by her small casket one by one, many of them said, "She looks like a little doll."
10 After the funeral mass, Carmen's father, Roberto, put the small wooden coffin on his shoulder. Then, with his wife behind him, he led the silent, single-file procession to the cemetery on the hill outside the village.

A few days later, Carmen's mother, Rosa, put all the little girl's
15 clothes and playthings in a small box and gave them to a priest from another village. When her husband, Roberto, came home from the field that evening, she said to him, "I gave away Carmen's things today."

"You did?" he said with a look of surprise.

"Yes, I did," Rosa replied. I gave them to the priest from one of the
20 villages down the valley. He was glad to have them for . . ."

"But why didn't you save them for a while, at least?" Roberto interrupted.

"There's no reason to save them," she said, as she stood in front of

him and took his rough hands. "You know what the doctor said after I
gave birth to Carmen."   25

Tears came to the man's eyes as he held her close. "I know very well
what the doctor told you. But he doesn't know everything. Only God
knows who can and can't have children." His voice cracked with emotion as he added, "I still have hope."

Rosa stepped back and looked into her husband's eyes. "My dear   30
Roberto, it's good to have hope, but false hope is not good. It's true that
the doctor doesn't know everything, but you know that in these four
years . . ."

"In these four years," he interrupted, "you had your hands full with a
sick child. God knew that. That's why He didn't send us another child."   35

Rosa didn't know what to say. She sat down at the table and put her
head in her hands. Roberto walked over to the window and looked out
to the backyard where little Carmen often played. Then he turned to
Rosa and asked, "Did you give away the little doll, too? The one Carmen always had in her hands?"   40

As she raised her head and looked at her husband, Rosa said, "No,
Roberto, that doll wasn't with her other things."

"It wasn't?" he asked with a look of surprise on his face.

"No, I'm sure it wasn't! I wonder what happened to it."

"I remember that she had it in her hand when she clsoed her eyes the 45
last time."

"Yes, you're right; she did. But what happened to it after that?"

They looked everywhere in their little house but could not find the
doll. They also asked friends, the neighborhood children, and even the
undertaker. No one knew anything about the lost doll. Roberto and   50
Rosa talked about it for weeks, but they never did find it.

Soon, however, they forgot about the lost doll. They had something
else to think about. The doctor, who said four years earlier that Rosa
couldn't have any more children, found out that he was wrong.

On the first anniversary of the death of little Carmen, Rosa gave birth 55
to another baby girl. It was a very happy occasion. With the child in her
arms, Rosa said to her husband, "I think God gave our baby back to us.
She even looks like Carmen."

At the baby's baptism they named her Evangelina, which the priest
told them meant "good news."   60

As Evangelina grew, she looked more and more like her sister, Carmen. Her actions and her character were similar to Carmen's, too. The
big difference was that Evangelina was healthy.

One day when Evangelina was about two years old, the parish priest
65 said to Rosa, as he watched Evangelina play, "Rosa, sometimes I think
that God took your sick child, healed her, and gave her back to you."

"It seems that way, doesn't it?" answered Rosa. "This child is so
much like Carmen!"

One day, when Evangelina was almost four, she said to her mother,
70 "I was very sick a long time ago, wasn't I, mommá?"

"No my child," Rosa answered with a smile, "*you* weren't sick. Your
sister, Carmen, was."

"But mommá," the child insisted, "I know I was sick!"

"No, my child," she said, as she took her by the hand, "you were not
75 sick a long time ago and you are not sick now. You are in good health. I
thank God for that."

"But I remember, mommá! I remember!"

"I think we talk about your sister too much, Evangelina. That's what
makes you think *you* were the one who was sick."

80 A few days later, Rosa's sister came to visit from Bogatá. The two
sisters talked together about many things. Once, when little Evangelina
came into the room, Rosa's sister said, "How much she looks like the
child you lost, Rosa!"

"Yes," replied Rosa, "and Evangelina not only *looks* like her sister
85 but also *is* like her in every way. The difference, of course, is that
Evangelina is healthy and well."

Evangelina listened to her mother and aunt as they spoke about her.
She then walked over to her aunt and said, "Auntie, I was sick a long
time ago, but now I am well. I thank God for that."

90 "I'm sure Evangelina hears us talk about her sister too much. Now
she thinks *she* was the one who was sick," Rosa said to her sister.

The little girl started to cry. "I *was* sick, auntie. I *know* I was! And I
remember that I had a dollie with blue eyes and a red dress!"

Rosa smiled. "Imagine that!" she said to her sister. "Evangelina even
95 remembers what someone said the little doll looked like."

"By the way," asked Rosa's sister, "did you ever find the little doll
that Carmen always had with her?"

"No, we didn't, she answered. "We don't know what happened to it."

Little Evangelina's eyes opened wide. "Now I remember, mommá!"
100 she exclaimed excitedly. "I remember where I put that dollie!"

"Where *you* put it?" laughed Rosa. "My dear, dear child, that dollie
was not *yours*! You never saw it in your life!"

"But I did, mommá! I did! That dollie was mine when I was sick. And

I didn't know what to do with it, so I put it under the big tree in the
yard!"   105

Evangelina took her mother and aunt by the hand, and together they
walked into the backyard. "It's right here under this big tree!" she
exclaimed, as she pointed to the hard, stony ground next to the tree.
"Dig it up, mommá! Dig it up! It's right under here!"

The sisters looked at each other. Neither knew what to say. Then, for   110
some reason, Rosa took a shovel from nearby and started to dig. A few
inches under the ground they saw what appeared to be the arm of a doll.
Rosa's heart pounded as she carefully dug deeper. In a minute she took
the doll from its shallow grave and shook off the dirt. She couldn't
believe her eyes. Evangelina jumped for joy. "I told you, mommá! I told 115
you it was there! Didn't I, auntie?"

Rosa didn't know what to say. She looked at her sister and then
turned to Evangelina and said, "My child, please tell me who put this
dollie in the ground here. And tell me how *you* knew it was there?"

"*I* put it there, mommá! I really *did*! I remember now. I really *do*!" 120

Rosa couldn't say another word. Then her sister said to the little girl,
"Tell us more, Evangelina. Tell us everything you remember."

"Well," the child began, "I remember that I was very sick. The priest
came and prayed with his hand on my head. Then I went to sleep. Then
somebody *woke me up*! A real nice man woke me up and took me by the   125
hand. But when he saw the dollie in my other hand, he said, 'I'm sorry,
but you can't take that with you. You don't need it now,' or something
like that. So I asked him if I could bury the dollie in the yard. He said
'yes' and helped me put it under the ground, here under this tree. He
didn't even have a shovel."   130

Then little Evangelina looked up at her mother. "Are you all right,
mommá?" she asked. "You look kind of sick."

A.   Questions on content.

   1. What was Carmen's *full* name?
   2. Describe Carmen.
   3. How old was the little girl when she died?
   4. What were Mr. and Mrs. Soto's first names?
   5. To whom did Rosa give Carmen's clothes and playthings?
   6. Which special plaything did Roberto ask about?
   7. How long after Carmen's death did Rosa give birth to another
       child?

8. Why did they name the new baby Evangelina?
9. How were Carmen and Evangelina alike?
10. In what way were they different?
11. Where did Rosa's sister live?
12. Where did they finally find the lost doll?
13. Who, did Evangelina say, helped her put it there?

B.   Vocabulary practice.

1. Choose the correct answer.
   a. Carmen died a few days after she *turned four*, which means that she died (shortly after her fourth birthday/four days later/on the fourth of the month).
   b. They passed by her coffin *one by one*, which means that (only one went/they went one at a time/they had a procession).
   c. In the *single-file* procession which Roberto led (only single people marched/they marched behind each other in a line/they walked side by side).
   d. When Rosa said, "*False hope* is not good," she meant that (it is not good to wish for the impossible/it is not good to tell lies/God knows what is right).
   e. When Roberto said Rosa *had her hands full* with little Carmen, he meant that she (couldn't have more children/she was very busy with the one child she had/the doctor didn't know everything).
   f. When Roberto said that little Carmen had the doll in her hand *when she closed her eyes the last time*, he meant that (she always had it when she fell asleep/the doll helped Carmen go to sleep/she had it when she died).
   g. If Evangelina *looked like* her sister, she had (a similar character/similar physical features/similar actions).
   h. If the ground under the tree was *hard and stony*, it appeared that (someone dug there before/no one dug there before/the doll was there).
   i. Rosa's *heart pounded* as she dug up the doll because (digging is hard work/the little girl jumped for joy/she was nervous).
   j. Rosa *looked sick* when Evangelina explained what she remembered because (this all seemed too mysterious/she had a headache/she didn't believe Evangelina).

2. Match the words which have more or less the *same* meaning.

a. ill	**1.** well
b. frail	**2.** weak
c. healthy	**3.** happy
d. glad	**4.** good
e. little	**5.** sick
f. similar	**6.** small
g. close	**7.** alike
	8. near

3. Match the *opposites*.

a. give	**1.** receive
b. come	**2.** lose
c. stand	**3.** visit
d. find	**4.** go
e. forget	**5.** stop
f. start	**6.** dig up
g. wake up	**7.** sit
h. bury	**8.** remember
	9. go to sleep

C.   Practice with the past tense.

Choose the correct word.

1. Carmen (die/died) when she was four years old.
2. When the people passed by her casket, they (think/thought) Carmen looked like a little doll.
3. After the funeral, Roberto (lead/led) the procession to the cemetery.
4. Rosa didn't (give/gave) away the doll.
5. Roberto thought of the doll when he (look/looked) out the window.
6. Roberto and Maria didn't (know/knew) what happened to the doll.
7. Maybe they (asks/asked) the priest for a special name for their new baby.
8. I don't think the priest (believe/believed) in reincarnation.
9. Last week, Rosa's sister from Bogatá (visit/visited) her.
10. When she told them where to dig, they (dig/dug) up the doll.
11. When they found the doll, Evangelina (jumps/jumped) for joy.
12. Evangelina said that when the nice man woke her up, she (has/had) the doll in her hand.

13. She said the nice man (bury/buried) the doll for her.
14. Rosa was so nervous, she (can't/couldn't) speak.
15. When Evangelina turned to her mother, she (see/saw) a strange look on her face.

D.   Questions for discussion.

(Divide into small groups if the class is large.)

1. Why, do you suppose, almost everyone in the village attended Carmen's funeral?
2. Why, in some countries, do they bury the dead *within one day* after the person's death?
3. What indications are there in the story that the Soto family was Roman Catholic?
4. Do you think there were any vehicles in the funeral procession? Explain.
5. Why do you suppose the people marched *single-file* to the cemetery?
6. What indications are there in the story that the Soto family was poor?
7. Why, do you think, Rosa gave Carmen's things to someone from another village? (Why didn't she give them to a neighbor or the priest in her own village?)
8. Why did Roberto want to save Carmen's things?
9. Why did Rosa say that there was no reason to save them?
10. Rosa said to her husband, "False hope is not good." When does hope become *false*? How can we know when hope is false?
11. What did Rosa want to say when she said to her husband, "You know that in these four years . . ."? Finish the sentence for her.
12. Why do you think Roberto thought of Carmen's doll when he looked out the window to the backyard?
13. What made them finally forget about the lost doll?
14. Do you think Evangelina was a good name for the new baby? Explain.

E.   More speaking practice (in small groups, if possible).

1. Tell the story in your own words. (One person can begin, another continue, and so on.)

2. The story "The Recurring Dream" uses only the present tense. Read the story again and change it to the past tense. Begin like this:

Kimberly Clark, who lived and worked in London, England, seemed like a normal young woman of twenty-five. She was pretty, she loved to dance, and she had many friends. Also, she had a good position in the office of a large company.

F.   Writing practice.

1. Look up the word *reincarnation*. Then write your definition and explanation of the word.
2. Write a paragraph in answer to one of the following:
   a. Do you think Rosa believed in reincarnation when she said at Evangelina's birth, "I think God gave us our baby back?" Explain.
   a. Do you think the parish priest believed in reincarnation when he said to Rosa, "Sometimes I think God took your child, healed her, and gave her back to you?" Explain.
3. Write a paragraph about the similarity (likeness) between the *lost doll* and *Carmen herself*.
4. Imagine that you sent a copy of this story to your father or mother with your last letter and asked for their comment. Then write what you think would be his or her answer to you.
5. Write what you think Rosa told her husband, Roberto, about how they found the lost doll. (Or write the conversation you think they had when she told him about how they found the doll.)

G.   A bit of humor,

A student from Panama told me this story.

A Twentieth-Century Fable

One day a house cat chased a mouse across the floor. The mouse ran as fast as he could and narrowly escaped into his hole in the corner of the room.

Safe in his hole, the mouse wiped his brow and said, "I didn't know they had a new cat. Boy, he is fast!"

While he thought about how he got away from the new cat, the mouse felt very proud of himself. "I'm really a very clever fellow, if I have to say so myself," he said. "No cat is as clever as I am!"

Just then he heard, "Arf! Arf!" and the scream of the cat out in the living room. The mouse jumped for joy. "Oh boy! Oh boy!" he exclaimed. "The dog is after the cat! I have to go and see that stupid cat run!"

The mouse scampered out of his hole into the room and looked, but he did not see the dog or the cat. Then, all of a sudden, WHAM! Something came from behind and slammed down on his tail. Before he could turn around, the mouse felt himself between two paws with sharp claws.

"Oh no!" he said, as he looked up into the piercing eyes of the cat. "How can this be? I heard the bark and the scream, and I thought the dog . . ."

"It pays to be bilingual," interrupted the cat, as he looked down at the mouse and smiled.

The House Call

Based on a story told by Hans Braun of Germany.

It was the day after Christmas, 1903, 9:30 in the evening. The famous German surgeon, Dr. Emil Braun, was sitting alone in the dining room of his apartment in the heart of the city of Berlin. For more than eight hours that day he performed and supervised difficult surgical opera-
5   tions. Now, late in the evening, he was trying to write notes about the surgery while he was attempting to eat his dinner. The elderly doctor was, however, too tired to do either. Soon he dozed off with his head on his arm on the table.

He woke up suddenly when he heard the doorbell ring. Then he
10   heard his wife say, "The doctor is resting, little girl. Is it all right if he goes to see your mother in the morning?"

The doctor heard the weak but clear voice of a child answer, "My mother is very, very sick. I think she's dying."

Dr. Braun got up slowly and went to the door. There, in the semi-
15   darkness of the doorway, stood a thin, little girl of perhaps six or seven. She was wearing a cotton dress and shabby shoes. Over her head she had a ragged shawl which she was holding together at the neck. Looking down sympathetically, the doctor asked her, "Where is your mother, child?"

20   She smiled weakly as she answered, "Come. I can show you. It's not far."

As Mrs. Braun helped her husband put on his coat, she said, "You work so hard all day in surgery, Emil, my dear. Why do you go out like this at night?"

"I do whatever God puts in front of me, my dear," he replied, "and right now I have a house call to make. You heard the little girl; her sick mother is waiting for me." His wife shook her head as the doctor put on his hat, picked up his little black bag, and went out into the night.

It was raining lightly as he walked down the steps to the street. The little girl was already almost a block up the street, waiting for him. When she saw him coming, she turned around and walked quickly toward the corner. Stopping only long enough to see that the doctor was coming, she turned. Then, continuing to walk nearly a half a block ahead, she led the doctor through the poorest part of Berlin, the section of the city around the hospital where Dr. Braun was head surgeon. He hurried through the streets the best he could for his age, trying to catch up to the little girl so he could ask her a few questions. She walked too fast, however, stopping only for a moment at each corner to make sure he saw where she was going.

Finally the little girl came to an old tenement house. Entering the dark, front hallway, she started up the stairs. Dr. Braun followed. Again he tried to catch up, but the child was almost up the second flight of stairs before he stood at the top of the first. She almost seemed to fly up five stories, pausing only long enough at the top of each flight of stairs to see that the doctor was coming. As he puffed along behind her, the elderly doctor thought of how much easier it was for him to run up stairs like this when he started his practice forty years earlier. He was only twenty-seven then. "But I can still do it!" he said to himself, as he finally stood at the top of the stairs on the fifth floor.

As the doctor caught his breath, he looked around and saw the little girl standing in front of a doorway at the end of the dark hallway. "She's in here, sir," the little girl said, pointing through the doorway. "And sir," she said as he walked past her, "thank you. Thank you very much. You are a very kind man."

"And thank you, child," he answered. "You are a very obedient little girl to let your mother send you out on a cold, rainy night like this." As the doctor entered the room, he heard the door close softly behind him.

In the dim light, the doctor saw a woman lying in the only bed in the small room. When he came closer, he recognized her as a person who at one time worked on the maintenance staff at the hospital.

It was easy for the doctor to see that the woman was suffering from pneumonia. He gave her some medicine and tried to make her as comfortable as possible. Then, he pulled up a chair and sat down by the bed and spoke softly to her. "I didn't know you were back in the city, Elda.

25

30

35

40

45

50

55

60

65

It was about three years ago that you went to live in the country with your brother, wasn't it?"

"Yes, it was, Dr. Braun," she said, trying to smile. "I came back to Berlin three months ago, right after my little girl . . ."

70 "Your little girl is so much bigger, Elda," he interrupted. "How time passes!"

"My little girl?" she asked weakly.

"Yes, the one you sent to get me tonight. You have only one child, don't you?"

75 "I *had* one child, doctor. Adelheid was her name." She looked into the kind face of the doctor as she went on slowly. "My little daughter died of the flu in September. If this is the twenty-sixth," she continued, "Heide passed away just three months ago today, three days after her seventh birthday."

80 The doctor had a look of surprise on his face as he looked around the room. The little girl was not there.

"I have Heide's shoes and shawl over there to remind me of her," the sick woman said, feebly pointing to the corner of the room. "She was such a beautiful child. When I see her shoes and shawl, it almost seems

85 like she's still here with me."

The doctor got up and looked. There on a hook was a ragged shawl like the one the little girl wore. And on the floor beneath was a small pair of shabby shoes. As he looked more closely, he saw that the shoes were wet. A cold chill went down his spine when he felt the shawl and

90 found that it, too, was damp.

"The shoes and shawl are there, Dr. Braun, aren't they?" she asked in a hoarse whisper.

"Yes, Elda, they are. They're here, just like you said."

"You see, then, there was some mistake about who went to get you

95 tonight, wasn't there?"

"Yes, Elda. Yes, I'm sure there was," he answered softly, while staring at the shawl and shoes.

"It's strange," she said slowly, "I was thinking about you earlier tonight, hoping . . . praying . . . that . . . that . . ."

100 The doctor turned around and saw that the sick woman was asleep. Then, after touching her feverish head once more, he took his black bag, stepped out into the dark hallway, and closed the door.

A. Questions on the content of the story.

1. How long ago did this story take place?
2. What was the doctor doing when the doorbell rang?

3. Who answered the door?
4. Who came to the door asking for the doctor?
5. Why did the little girl come to the doctor's home?
6. Where did the sick woman live?
7. How old was Dr. Braun when this took place? (See line 45 and following.)
8. To which floor of the tenement house did the little girl lead Dr. Braun?
9. What sickness did the woman have?
10. Where did Elda live for three years before she returned to Berlin?
11. What was the little girl's name? What did her mother call her?
12. How old was the little girl when she died?
13. What did the mother keep to remind her of her daughter?

B. Vocabulary practice.

Choose the correct answer.

1. The doctor was *attempting* to eat his dinner, which means (the dinner was very tempting/he was trying to eat/he was too tired).
2. The doctor *dozed off* at the table, which means (he fell asleep/he fell off/he ate his dinner).
3. The little girl stood in the *semidarkness* of the doorway, which means (she was a ghost/she had dark clothes on/she stood where there was not much light).
4. The doctor looked at the little girl *sympathetically*, which means (he felt sorry for her/he knew her mother/he knew there was something strange about her).
5. The doctor said he had a *house call* to make, which means (he had to go to someone's home to help the person/he had to make a telephone call/he had to go out into the night).
6. The doctor was trying to *catch up* with the little girl, which means (he wanted to ask her some questions/he was not as young as he used to be/he was attempting to walk fast enough to get where she was).
7. Dr. Braun *recognized* the sick woman, which means (she at one time worked at the hospital/he knew who she was/he treated her).
8. Heide *passed away* three months earlier, which means (she died/she was sick/she became a ghost).
9. The woman kept Heide's shoes and shawl *to remind* her of her

daughter, which means (when she saw those things, she thought of Heide/they were things which belonged to Heide/she didn't want to give them away).

10. A *cold chill went down the doctor's spine* when he felt the shawl and found that it was damp, perhaps because (the little girl was not there/this all seemed very strange/it was very cold in the room).

C. Practice with the past tense.

Write each sentence, changing it to the past tense.

Example: The story takes place in Berlin.
  The story took place in Berlin.

1. The doctor lives in Berlin.

  _____

2. He is a famous surgeon.

  _____

3. The girl rings the doorbell and waits.

  _____

4. The doctor's wife does speak to the girl.

  _____

5. Mrs. Braun does not want him to go.

  _____

6. The doctor can't catch up with the girl.

  _____

7. The little girl flies up the stairs.

  _____

8. The doctor does want to help.

  _____

9. Heide thanks the doctor.

  _____

10. Dr. Braun knows this woman.

  _____

11. The woman and the doctor do speak together.

  _____

12. Elda comes back to Berlin.

_____

13. The shawl feels damp.

_____

D.   Practice with the progressive.

Change the *present* and *past tenses* of the verbs in italics to the progressive form. Take care to notice the tense.

Examples: The doctor *eats* late at night.
              The doctor is eating late at night.
              The doorbell *rang*.
              The doorbell was ringing.

1. The doctor *tried* to write notes.

_____

2. Heide *stands* in the doorway.

_____

3. The girl *wore* a shawl on her head.

_____

4. The doctor's wife *helped* him with his coat.

_____

5. The doctor and the little girl *walk* in the rain.

_____

6. The girl *looks* back at the doctor.

_____

7. The doctor *caught* up with her.

_____

8. He *gave* her some medicine.

_____

9. The little girl *died* of the flu.

_____

10. The woman *fell* asleep.

_____

E. Questions for discussion (in small groups, if possible).

    1. If the doctor was too tired to eat or write, why was he *not* too tired to go to see the sick woman?

    2. Why do you think the little girl walked ahead of the doctor instead of walking *with* him?

    3. The story says that the doctor was trying to catch up with the little girl so he could ask her a few questions.

      a. What do you think he wanted to ask her?

      b. Do you think the girl wanted to answer questions? Explain.

    4. Dr. Braun interrupted the sick woman when she said, "I came back to Berlin three months ago, right after my little girl. . . ." What do you think she was trying to say?

    5. Why did the doctor have a look of surprise on his face when Elda told him that her little girl died in September?

    6. Elda said, "When I see Heide's shoes and shawl, it almost seems like she's still here with me." What do you think the doctor was thinking when he heard her say that?

    7. Do you think it's a good idea to keep reminders of lost loved ones like Elda did? Explain.

    8. What do you think the doctor thought when he found out that the shoes were wet and the shawl damp?

    9. Elda fell asleep while she was saying, "It's strange. I was thinking about you earlier tonight, hoping . . . praying . . . that . . . that. . . ." What do you think she was trying to say?

    10. Do you think Elda's hoping and praying had anything to do with the doctor's coming to see her? Explain.

    11. Why do you suppose the doctor did not tell Elda *that night* what happened?

    12. Do you think he told her *later?* Explain.

F. Storytelling.

    1. Tell the story in your own words. (One person can begin, then point to another in the group to continue, and so on.)

    2. Tell the group a "ghost story," or tell about an appearance-after-death that you know about.

G. Writing practice.

    1. Write a paragraph describing Dr. Braun.

    2. Write what you think Dr. Braun told his wife when he returned from this house call, or write the conversation which took place when he told her.

3. Write a paragraph explaining why you think Dr. Braun *did* or *did not* tell Elda *later* what happened that night.

4. Write a paragraph explaining why you *do* or *do not* believe that people sometimes appear after death, like in this story.

5. Write about an experience (yours or someone else's) with someone who appeared after death.

H. Reading practice.

With another person in the class, read this dialogue *aloud, with feeling.*

Dr. Braun: I didn't know you were back in the city, Elda. You went to live in the country three years ago, didn't you?

Elda: Yes, I did, Dr. Braun. But I came back to Berlin three months ago, right after my little girl . . .

Dr. Braun: Your little girl is so much bigger now.

Elda: My little girl?

Dr. Braun: Yes, the one who came to get me tonight.

Elda: There must be some mistake. Heide, my only child, died in September.

I. A bit of humor.

There are many humorous stories about doctors. Here are a few which I hope you will enjoy.

1. A doctor received a call in the night which the caller said was urgent. "Doc!" he began frantically. "This is Matti Jorgenson. You have to come right away; my wife is sick with appendicitis!"

"It can't be appendicitis, Matti, you see . . ."

"It's appendicitis, Doc, I know it is! I know from experience!"

"But I took your wife's appendix out two years ago. Don't you remember?"

"Yes, I remember, Doc; that's how I got the experience. Now I have a different wife."

2. Some years ago, on a cold winter night, a veterinarian in a small town in the Ozark Mountains of Missouri heard a knock on the door. When he opened it, he saw an old farmer standing there whom he knew.

"Can you go to my place right away, Doc? It's very important."

"All right, if you give me a few minutes to get ready."

"The farmer waited. Then, when the doctor was ready, he said to him, "Is it okay if I ride along?"

"Certainly. Jump in!" the doctor replied, and they were off.

When they arrived at the man's farm, back in the hills, the doctor asked, "Is it one of your cows, Joe?"

"No it's not, Doc. It's just that I didn't have a ride home." Then he handed a five-dollar bill to the doctor and said, "Here you are, Doc. That greedy taxi driver in town wanted seven dollars to drive out here, and I knew you charged only five, if what you had to do wasn't too complicated."

3.   A cranky old man came into a doctor's office one fall day, shaking his fist.

"Calm down, Jake!" said the physician, who knew the man well. "Have a seat and tell me what's wrong."

The old man sat down. Then he leaned forward and pointed his finger at the doctor. "Last winter, you know, I came in here with bronchitis and you gave me some medicine."

"It took care of the bronchitis, didn't it, Jake? I remember seeing you in the street a number of times since then, looking pretty healthy."

"But you have to guarantee your work longer than that, Doc. That's less than a year ago and here I am coughing and sneezing again."

Meet Death!

Based on the "Pardoner's Tale" in the Canterbury Tales *by Geoffrey Chaucer.*

One morning three drunken men were sitting in a tavern. As they drank and talked together, they heard a churchbell toll. One of them said to a boy who worked in the tavern, "Go and see whose funeral that is."

"I already know, sir," replied the boy, "and I hope what I am going to
5 tell you will not surprise you."

"Why do you say that?"

"Because the person who's on his way to the cemetery in a coffin this morning is your old comrade, Caleb."

"Really? How did he die?" the man asked.

10 "I hope this will not shock you too much either: That sneaky thief, Death, knocked him off a tavern stool last night."

"Death did that?"

"Yes, sir. He took the poor man's life right there in front of his friends. At least, that's what someone said."

15 The tavernkeeper heard the conversation. "The boy is right!" he said. "Death killed the man dead! I heard that, too."

"Who's this fellow, Death?" asked the man as he took another drink of ale.

"No one sees him," answered the tavernkeeper. "But I think he lives
20 somewhere nearby because he kills so many people around here. Men, women, and children! Rich and poor!"

"And, sir," added the boy, "unless someone does something about it, I think Death is going to kill all of us."

"The boy is right!" cried another of the drunken men. "Death will soon kill us all. Somebody has to do something. But who will do it?"   25

"*We* will!" shouted the third man, as he jumped up, pointing a knife, as though ready to kill the next man who came through the door.

"*You* will?" said the tavernkeeper in disbelief.

"Yes, *we* will!" he replied. Then he put his arms around his two friends and said, "Won't we, my friends?"   30

"But what will we do?" asked one of them.

"We'll kill *him*, of course!" he laughed. "Look, we'll make an agreement, the three of us, that we will not come back to this house of friendship until we find Death and kill him dead. How about it?"

The other two agreed. Then all three men laughed and shook hands   35 over their pact, as they staggered out of the tavern together. As they left, the tavernkeeper called, "I hope you're not going to stay away too long!"

"We aren't!" they replied. "We're coming back as soon as we take care of this guy, Death!"   40

As they walked together out of the village, one of the men asked the others, "What will we do when we find Death?"

"I know!" replied another, using his hands and body to demonstrate, "Whoever recognizes him first will say, 'Meet Death!' And when he puts out his hand and says, 'How do you do?' we'll all put our knives into   45 his body, two in the sides and one in the middle!" Then, with a look of satisfaction, he said, "What do you think of that?"

"Good plan!" said the other two.

Just then, as the three came to the first crossroad, they met a mysterious looking man. He carried a long walking stick and wore a long,   50 black robe with a hood which almost hid his face. He turned toward the men, letting them see his wrinkled face and sunken eyes.

"Who are you?" asked one of the men, looking him straight in the eye.

"My name is Old Age," he replied.   55

"What do you do with the stick?"

"I tap the earth as I walk from one end of the land to the other, hoping that someday Death will be kind enough to let me in, and . . ."

"Did you say, 'Death'?" interrupted another of the men.

"Yes, I did. Why do you ask?"   60

"Because that's the fellow we're looking for."

"You want to find Death?" asked the old man, looking down as he spoke softly.

"Yes, we do!" shouted one of the three angrily.

65 "And what will you do when you find him?"

"We'll kill him!" he replied, pointing his knife toward the old man.

"Why?"

"Because he's killing so many people around here."

"Just yesterday," added another, "he killed a friend of ours who was
70 just having a good time with his friends." He tried to make a tear come
to his eye as he went on, "We're men with good hearts. Men of good
will. We want to help our fellowmen by killing Death."

"I can see what kind of men you are," said the old man. "And for that
reason I'm going to help you find Death."

75 "I hope you're telling us the truth, old man!" yelled one of the men,
as he grabbed him by the throat. "Or we'll separate your head from your
shoulders and give it to the birds!"

"Please show more respect for me," gasped the man. "I shall indeed
tell you the truth. The painful truth."

80 "So, tell us!" said the man roughly as he pushed him.

"Do you want to meet Death *today?*" asked the old man with a
sympathetic look on his face.

"Yes, today!" they all said. "Tell us where he is!"

"If you want to meet Death today, please listen carefully to what I am
85 going to say." Then the old man leaned on his walking stick with one
hand and pointed with the other as he said, "Follow this path into the
forest until you arrive at an old well. Take the path to the left there,
until you come to a large rock. Go right from that rock about ten steps
into the brush. There you will see a very large oak tree. You shall indeed
90 find Death there. He will be sitting behind that tree."

"Are you sure about that?" asked one of the men as he took hold of
the old man again.

"Very sure!" he replied. "In fact," he added, "Death is having a party
later this afternoon for a few friends. If you hurry, perhaps you will be
95 able to attend. About the time you arrive, he'll be waiting behind that
oak tree for his guests."

"I hope you are telling us the truth, old one!" said one of the men.
"Because if you are not, we shall return and end your miserable life!"

"You heard the truth from me just now. So, if you will follow my
100 instructions, I know that you will meet Death. 'Seek and you shall find,'
says the Good Book."

The three men left. And although they argued at each place about
which way to turn, they finally found the big oak tree. Stealthily, they
went around it from both directions with their knives in hand.

105 To their great surprise, instead of discovering a person behind the

tree, they found some large baskets of gold coins. Eight in all!

"Whose money do you suppose this is?" asked one, with his eyes wide open in surprise.

"What do you mean 'whose money'?" cried another. "Who's here with it? It's ours, you idiot! It's a gift from God for three men who are down on their luck!" Then all three of them laughed happily as they ran their greedy hands through the gold coins. From that moment on, they completely forgot about their search for Death.

"My friends," said one of them, "we have enough money here so that none of us will have to work again another day. But we can't, of course, take it to our homes now. We will have to wait till dark so that people won't see us. Otherwise they'll think we stole it."

"You're right!" said another.

"Well, then," said the third, "if we're waiting till tonight to take our treasure home, we'll need some bread and wine to make the hours go by faster, won't we?"

"Indeed we will!" said another. "Let's draw straws to see who will go back to the village. The other two will stay and guard the money."

They all agreed. Then the one who lost the draw left for the village. As he walked along, he thought to himself, "if I can somehow do away with those two no-good bums, I will have all that gold for myself, and no one will know where I got it." Then he smiled as an idea came to his intoxicated mind.

In the village he bought the bread and wine. Then he went to a chemist and purchased some powerful rat poison. When he left the village again, he went behind a tree and put the poison into the wine.

Meanwhile, the two who were waiting for him covered the baskets of gold coins with leaves and sticks. Then one of them said to the other, "Good brother, it's too bad we can't divide this gold *two* ways rather than three."

"Why can't we?" asked the other. "Two are stronger than one. Really, friend, I think we will be doing a service to humanity if we end the miserable life of that worthless bum."

So, when the man returned from the village, the two jumped on him. He didn't have a chance. They murdered him in cold blood and threw his lifeless body into the bushes. "The animals will take care of his corpse tonight," said one.

"I hope they won't get too drunk on his blood," laughed the other. Then he slapped his knee with his hat and said, "Let's celebrate, comrade. Just think. We'll never have to work another day of our lives!"

"Right." said the other. "And isn't it nice that our friend brought us bread and wine for our celebration?" Then they sat down together under the oak tree. And, of course, they began to celebrate by drinking their fill of the wine which their comrade mixed especially for them.

A.   Questions on the content of the story.

    1. How did the men know that there was a funeral?
    2. Where were they when they heard the bell?
    3. According to the boy, who killed the man?
    4. What did the three men agree to do?
    5. Describe the man they met at the crossroad.
    6. What did the three men tell the old man when he asked why they wanted to kill Death?
    7. Where did the old man say they could find Death?
    8. What did they discover behind the tree?
    9. Whose money did they decide it was?
    10. Why didn't they take the money home immediately?
    11. Why did they want someone to go back to the village?
    12. How did they decide which one should go?
    13. Why did the man go to the chemist's shop in the village?
    14. What did he do with what he bought?
    15. What happened to him when he returned to his two friends?
    16. How did the other two celebrate?

B.   Vocabulary practice.

    1. Underline the correct answer.
        a. The men heard a churchbell *toll*, which means they heard (a bell ring/a bell ring slowly, at regular intervals/a bell ring beautifully).
        b. The bell tolled for a *funeral*, which means that it rang for (a special service for a person who died/a special service for a cemetery/a special service for a comrade).
        c. The tavernkeeper spoke *in disbelief*. That was because (he didn't think they could do what they said/he didn't want them to kill Death/he believed them).
        d. The men *shook hands over their pact*, which showed that (they were happy to do this together/they liked each other/they were in agreement).
        e. One of the men told the old man that they were *men of*

good will, which means that he wanted him to believe that they were (men of God/men with good intentions/men who will do good).

f. The old man had a *sympathetic look* on his face when he spoke to the men, which showed that (he felt sorry for them/he wanted to help them find Death/he knew they were men of good will).

g. The verse from the Bible, "Seek and you shall find," means (you always find something if you look long enough/you will find what you look for/it pays to look for things).

h. The men *drew straws* in order to (send/look for/choose) one to go to the village.

i. A *chemist* who sells drugs is a (shopkeeper/drug addict/pharmacist).

j. The two men murdered the third *in cold blood,* which means (he bled a lot when they killed him/it didn't bother them when they killed him/they killed him at night when it was cold).

k. After the two men killed the third, one of them said, "The animals will *take care of* his corpse tonight." What he meant was that the animals would (guard/eat/find) his body.

2. Match the words which have more or less the *same* meaning.

a. continue	1. yell	
b. return	2. come back	
c. shout	3. separate	
d. grab	4. kill	
e. buy	5. take hold of	
f. search	6. go on	
g. murder	7. look for	
h. arrive	8. come to	
	9. purchase	

3. The words *whose* and *who's* are homonyms. That is, their pronunciation is the same, although their meanings are different.

Whose means *of whom* or *belonging to whom.*
Who's is a contraction for *who is.* (*Who's* can also mean *who has,* which will appear later in this book.)

Both *whose* and *who's* appear in this story in two places:

Examples: Go and see *whose* funeral that is.
The person *who's* on his way to the cemetery is your old comrade, Caleb.
Whose money do you suppose this is?
Who's here with it?

Write *who's* or *whose* to complete the following sentences. Look again at the preceding explanation and examples, if necessary.

1. I wonder _____ money this is.

2. _____ book is that on the table?

3. _____ going with you to the party Saturday night?

4. I don't know _____ responsibility that is.

5. At _____ house are we going to meet?

6. _____ the girl standing by the door?

7. _____ daughter is she?

8. That's the girl _____ brother is in our class.

9. That's the girl _____ always asking questions.

10. Don't you know _____ supposed to be here?

11. _____ the man in the long robe?

12. He's the man _____ name is Old Age.

C. Grammar practice.

1. Change *am, is,* or *are going to* to *will* to indicate the future.

Examples: They *are going to* look for Death.
They *will* look for Death.
He *is going to* tell them.
He *will* tell them.

a. **Maybe this** *is going to* surprise you.

Maybe this _____ surprise you.

b. "I *am going to* find Death!" he shouted.

"I _____ find Death!" he shouted.

c. We *are* not *going to* come back until we find him.

We _____ come back until we find him.

d. I hope you *are* not *going to* stay away too long.

I hope you _____ stay away too long.

e. *Are* they really *going to* find what they're looking for?

_____ they really find what they're looking for?

2. Change *will* to *am, is,* or *are going to* to indicate the future.

Examples: You *will* find him soon.
You *are going to* find him soon.
You *won't* recognize him.
You *aren't going to* recognize him.

a. They *will not* come back till they find him.

They _____ come back till they find him.

b. The old man *will* help them find Death.

The old man _____ help them find Death.

c. Death *will* be waiting for you.

Death _____ be waiting for you.

d. "We *will not* work again!" he cried.

"We _____ work again!" he cried.

e. The animals *will* take care of his corpse.

The animals _____ take care of his corpse.

3. The *present progressive form* of the verb in English is sometimes used to indicate a *future idea*. Along with this form, there must be some *indication of a future time* in the sentence.

Examples: He's *having* a party later this afternoon.
We're *waiting* till tonight to take our treasure home.

The meaning of these sentences is:

He's *going to have* a party later this afternoon.
We're *going to wait* till tonight to take our treasure home.

Change each of the following from *the progressive with a future idea* to the *future* by using *going to*.

Examples: We are *having* a meeting tomorrow.
We are *going to have* a meeting tomorrow.
My friend is *helping* me with my English later this afternoon.
My friend is *going to help* me with my English later this afternoon.

a. We are *having* a test Friday.

We are _____ a test Friday.

b. I'm *leaving* home at the end of the summer.

I'm _____ home at the end of the summer.

c. Isn't he *attending* the university next semester?

Isn't he _____ the university next semester?

d. John is *changing* his major next year.

John is _____ his major next year.

e. Are they *driving* to the city tomorrow?

Are they _____ to the city tomorrow?

f. Are you *going* to the hospital to see him tonight?

Are you _____ to the hospital to see him tonight?

g. He's *paying* me back as soon as he gets his check.

He's _____ me back as soon as he gets his check.

h. I think they're *meeting* tomorrow again.

I think they're _____ tomorrow again.

4. Most Americans do not commonly use *shall* today in normal conversation to indicate the future. They use *going to* and *will* much more commonly. However, some people use *shall* for special emphasis. Also, people use *shall* in formal papers.

Examples: "You *shall*, indeed, get what you ask for!"
From an insurance policy: "The company *shall* not assume responsibility until all premiums are paid in full."

Can you find an example or two of the use of *shall* in a formal paper or document?

_____

_____

_____

D.   Questions for discussion.

1. This story is from the late fourteenth century. Do you think some people at that time actually thought of *death* as a *person*? Explain.
2. The boy said that Death knocked their friend off a tavern stool. What do you think was possibly the cause of his death?
3. The three men in the story shook hands when they made an agreement. Is it the custom in your culture to do this, too? (In what other situations do people in your culture shake hands?)
4. Why do you think the tavernkeeper said to the three men, "I hope you're not going to stay away too long?"
5. Who do you think the man was who said that his name was Old Age?
6. What did the old man mean when he said he tapped the earth with his stick, *hoping that Death would let him in?*
7. What do you think the old man was thinking when he said, "I can see what kind of men you are. And for that reason I'm going to help you find Death?" Explain.
8. Why do you think men of this type frequently think that others are not telling the truth?
9. Why do you think the old man had a *sympathetic look* on his face when he asked if they wanted to meet Death that day?
10. What did the old man mean when he said that Death was having a party that afternoon and was waiting for his guests behind the oak tree?
11. Why did the men forget about looking for Death when they found the money?
12. Is "Meet Death" a good title for this story? Explain.

E.   Storytelling.

1. Tell the story in your own words. (One person can start, then point to another person to continue, and so on.)
2. Tell the class a story you know about *greed* or about strange things that *intoxicated people* sometimes do.

F.   Writing practice.

1. The person who told this story wanted to teach a lesson. Write a paragraph telling what you think that lesson is.
2. If you can think of a story from your culture which teaches a similar lesson, write a paragraph about it.
3. Write a paragraph on the thought "Seek and you shall find."
4. Write a paragraph on the topic "What Greed Does to People."

G.   Reading practice.

Read this dialogue with another member of your class. Try to read it *with feeling.*

Man: Who are you?
Old Man: My name is Old Age.
Man: What do you do with the stick?
Old Man: I tap the earth as I walk, hoping that someday Death will be kind enough to let me in.
Man: Did you say 'Death'?
Old Man: Yes, I did. Why do you ask?
Man: Because that's the fellow we're looking for.
Old Man: You want to find Death?
Man: Yes, we do.
Old Man: And what will you do when you find him?
Man: Kill him, of course.

H.   A bit of humor and a word of wisdom.

1. There are many stories about intoxication. Have you heard these?
   a. One day a zoo attendant accidentally left the door open on a lion's cage. When the lion came out roaring, people ran in every direction. An intoxicated man stumbled over to the lion, took him by the mane, and led him back to his cage. When the superintendent of the zoo came to commend him for his bravery, the drunken man said, "Do— do you mean to—to tell me that thing was real?"

b. One day a man bought a very expensive "grandfather" clock. He strapped the large clock to his back and walked very carefully toward his home, for he did not want even one small scratch on the precious possession. As the man turned around the last corner, near his home, a drunken man stumbled into him, sending him and his clock smashing to the sidewalk.

"Look what you did to my beautiful clock!" the man shouted angrily.

The drunken man leaned against a building and looked down at the man whose broken clock was still on his back. Then he said, "Shay, mishter, why don't you wear a clock on your wrist like other people do?"

2. Maybe we should add here *a word of wisdom* about liquor from William Shakespeare: "O God! Think of how men put an enemy in their mouths to steal away their brains!"

There is also a Chinese saying which states that the big problem with liquor is that a *man takes a drink,* then *the drink takes a drink,* and then *the drink takes the man.*

Feast in
the Desert

Based on an incident told by Ahmed Al-Sager of Kuwait.

"Please be careful, my son," said Ali's father, as they embraced. "Remember that the drive to San'a is long. Rest along the way when you
become weary, and remember, if a stranger on the way needs help, help
him. And if someone needs a ride, take him with you. God blesses you
for such acts of kindness."   5

"I know, father, and I will do as you say," Ali replied. "Please don't
worry about me. The car is new, and I will be careful."

"Go then, my son," said the father embracing his son once more,
"and come back to me safe and sound."

As Ali drove his father's big car out of the city of Aden,* he felt like a   10
man. Think of it: His father was trusting him to take his car to deliver
some very important papers for him, and he was *only eighteen* years old!
Ali felt proud and happy that his father asked him to come with him to
Aden to represent his company for a year. Yes, it was difficult to be away
from his mother and his brothers and sisters, but he would see them   15
again soon when he and his father returned to Kuwait, their home
country. Right now he couldn't think about that. He was on an important mission for his father.

After driving through the mountains, out of South Yemen, he entered
the desert region of the country of Yemen. Even though he liked driving   20

*Aden, the capital city of South Yemen, is on the Gulf of Aden, to the south of Saudi Arabia.
San'a, the capital city of Yemen, is inland and to the north of Aden, perhaps a five- to six-hour drive
by car.

his father's powerful automobile, the drive became tiresome on the
long, straight stretches of road in this area.

Suddenly, Ali saw something in the distance which looked like it
might be a man. As Ali came closer, he saw that it *was* a man, a man in
25 the tribal dress of this region. At first he hesitated, but then he remembered the words of his father, "If a stranger needs help, give him help,
and if he needs a ride, take him along." He slowed the car to a stop
where the man stood.

"Do you need help?" asked Ali through the window of the car. He
30 was glad to see that the man was not much older than he, perhaps no
more than twenty-five.

"I am going to San'a. Do you have room for me?"

"Yes, of course," smiled Ali. "I have a lot of room, and I will be happy
to have you with me. Please get in the front seat here with me."

35 In a few minutes Ali was wondering how happy he was to have this
young man with him. He acted a little strange, and he did not seem to
want to talk. He did, at least, tell Ali that his name was Jasem and that
his father was a tribal sheik.

After the two drove together for an hour, Ali turned to Jasem and
40 said, "Are you hungry? I'm starving. Let's look for a place to eat."

Jasem looked around as though he were trying to figure out where
they were. Then he said, "Slow down here and turn right at the next
road, if you're hungry."

"Do you know of a place here? It looks like there is nothing but
45 barren hills and desert."

"Slow down and turn!" Jasem said almost in a demanding shout. "I'll
take you to my uncle's home. He is having a feast today for his family
and friends. We can eat with them."

Ali turned off the highway onto a very rough road and drove perhaps
50 five minutes. Then he turned to Jasem and said, "I don't think we can
make it much farther on this road with this car. It's too . . ."

"Go on!" interrupted Jasem in a loud voice. "We *can* make it and we
will!"

Ali did not want to offend the man, so he continued. Slowly they
55 moved on over a road that was obviously a road for carts, not cars. After
several more turns this way and that through the low hills, Ali stopped
the car and said, "I really don't think I should . . ."

"Keep going!" demanded Jasem. "It's just over the next hill."

Ali continued driving slowly up the hill. On the other side, to his
60 great surprise, he saw a beautiful oasis. There were palm trees and even
some small green fields. "What did I tell you?" said Jasem with a shake
of the head and a gesture of his hands.

They entered the oasis and found the people celebrating with a feast of all the best foods you could imagine. Jasem introduced Ali to his uncle and a number of other people. The people, perhaps twenty-five in all, 65 seemed very different to Ali, but they were friendly and tried in their own way to make him feel at home. Their dialect of Arabic was a little different, but Ali adapted quickly to it.

After a look at the beautiful tables of food, Ali forgot about how different these people were. When someone said, "Eat your fill," Ali 70 began. He ate and ate of the many different types of food. Soon his stomach hurt from eating so much.

Ali then saw that the sun was very low in the western sky. He remembered that he told his father that he would try to arrive in San'a before nightfall. Now it looked like that would be impossible, but he did want 75 to get on his way. He spoke to Jasem who said he wanted to go on with him to San'a, so Ali thanked his hosts and they left.

In the semidarkness of the evening the road was difficult to see. After driving for some time, when Ali thought they should be almost back to the highway, they came to a fork in the road. Ali turned right, which he 80 thought was correct, but suddenly Jasem sat up and shouted, "Go back! Take the road to the left!"

Ali stopped the car, but he didn't know what to do. On the one hand, he didn't want to argue with this strange young man. On the other hand, he was certain that *he* was right about which road to take and Jasem was 85 not.

Ali got out of the car and walked the short distance back to the place where he turned. Jasem followed.

"Look, Jasem!" he said, "our tracks are here on this road I took. There are no tire tracks on the other road. *This* is the way we came." 90

Jasem stared at Ali. Then he said angrily, "I don't care what you say about tracks! Take the other road!"

Although Ali wanted no trouble, he knew what he had to do. "I'm sorry, Jasem," he said, trying to sound as friendly as possible, "but I feel that I must take this road." Then he started toward the car as he added, 95 "My father's business partner is already waiting for me in San'a, so I must go."

"Go, then!" he shouted. "Have your way, but you will be sorry."

Ali felt afraid as he got in the car. He wanted to speed away, but he did not want to be unkind. So he sat and waited a few minutes, hoping 100 that Jasem would calm down and decide to come with him.

After a few minutes, Ali looked back and saw Jasem still standing in the road. Then, a few minutes later, he looked back again and saw no one. He got out of the car and walked back, but could not find him.

105   "What a mystery!" he thought to himself. "I wonder what happened to him."

     Ali looked down and saw what clearly looked like Jasem's footprints. He followed them for perhaps a hundred feet. Then, strangely, the footprints seemed to disappear. There was no evidence of backtracking 110 or leaving the road. The footprints just stopped.

     "Well, now," said Ali to himself, "a person can't just disappear into thin air." He had a sickly feeling when he thought of how very mysterious this all seemed.

     He felt fear in every bone in his body as he looked again at the 115 footprints which just ended, as though the person who made them ceased to exist or something!

     Then Ali had another feeling which seemed mysterious. He felt like he had nothing in his stomach. He put his hands on his middle. His stomach seemed *empty*, not full! "The food I just ate is gone!" he ex-120 claimed. "How can this be?"

     Ali felt a cold chill go down his spine as he walked back to the car.

    A.   Questions on the content of the story.

      1. Who asked Ali to drive to San'a for him?
      2. What was the purpose of the trip?
      3. Where did Ali's family live?
      4. Why did he and his father come to Aden?
      5. How long did they plan to stay in Aden?
      6. Why did Ali stop for the stranger?
      7. Why did Ali and Jasem turn off the highway?
      8. Why didn't Ali want to continue on the road Jasem told him to take?
      9. What did Jasem do each time Ali said he didn't want to continue?
    10. What did they finally find over the last hill?
    11. What made Ali forget how different the people were at this place?
    12. How much did Ali eat?
    13. What made Ali think that he should leave the oasis?
    14. What did Jasem do when Ali turned to the right at the fork in the road?
    15. What reason did Ali give to show that the way he turned was correct?
    16. What did Ali decide to do when Jasem insisted that they go the other way?

17. Why did Ali wait for a few minutes in the car?
18. What did Ali find when he went back to find Jasem?

B.   Vocabulary practice.
   1. Underline the best answer.
      a. Ali *hesitated* before he stopped for Jasem, which means that (he slowed down/he noticed the man's tribal clothes/ he held back, not knowing for a moment what to do).
      b. A *sheik* is (an Arab chief/a member of a tribe/a stranger).
      c. Ali said he was *starving*. He meant that (he was dying from lack of food/he felt very hungry/he wanted to stop to eat).
      d. Ali didn't want to *offend* Jasem, which means that he didn't want to (hurt his feelings/agree with him/go with him).
      e. An *oasis* is (a place where people have feasts/a fertile place in a desert/a desert home).
      f. When people tell you to *eat your fill*, they mean you should (eat something that is filling/eat your own food/eat as much as you want).
      g. *Nightfall* is more or less the same as (evening/night/ midnight).
      h. Ali thanked his *hosts*, which means that he expressed thanks to (Jasem/Jasem's uncle and his family/the servants at the oasis).
      i. A *fork* in the road is also called (a Y/a crossroad/a corner).
      j. Jasem *stared* at Ali, which means that he (was angry/ shouted in a loud voice/looked at him intently).
      k. Ali said, "What a *mystery?*" because what happened was (strange/impossible/unbelievable).
      l. When Ali saw that there was *no evidence of backtracking*, he saw that (there were no tracks turning back/there were no footprints at all/Jasem disappeared).
   2. Match the words or phrases which mean more or less the *same* thing.

a. embrace	1. have confidence
b. return	2. continue
c. trust	3. hold close
d. keep on	4. cease
e. enter	5. become peaceful
f. calm down	6. go back
	7. go in

3. Match the *opposites*.

a. careful	**1.** rested
b. weary	**2.** satisfied
c. powerful	**3.** smooth
d. strange	**4.** familiar
e. rough	**5.** mysterious
f. hungry	**6.** weak
	7. careless

C. Grammar practice.

1. Practice with commands.

Commands are very simple in English. The command is always the same as the verb itself, and there is no difference in number or in gender.

Examples: <u>Go</u> to the door, please, John.
<u>Go</u> to the door, please, boys.
<u>Go</u> to the door, please, Helen.
<u>Go</u> to the door, please, girls.

There are, of course, also negative commands.

Examples: Don't worry about me.
Please do not stop.

a. Find at least twelve of the many commands in this story. Then list them on the following blanks.

Examples: Please *be* careful, my son.
Remember that the drive to San'a is long.

1. _____

2. _____

3. _____

4. _____

5. _____

6. _____

7. _____

8. _____

9. _____

10. _____

11. _____

12. _____

b. There are many commands *on signs in public places, in directions,* and so on. Explain where you see commands like these and what they mean.

   1. KEEP OFF GRASS
   2. PAY CASHIER
   3. DO NOT OPEN PACKAGES
   4. DO NOT ENTER
   5. WASH IN COLD WATER ONLY
   6. DON'T WALK
   7. USE ELM AVENUE DETOUR
   8. DRY CLEAN ONLY
   9. DON'T LITTER
  10. USE CORRECT CHANGE ONLY
  11. KEEP OUT OF REACH OF CHILDREN
  12. USE ONLY AS DIRECTED
  13. REFRIGERATE AFTER OPENING
  14. PUSH
  15. CLOSE TIGHTLY

c. List other commands you see and where you see them.

1. _____

2. _____

3. _____

4. _____

5. _____

6. _____

d. List commands you hear in your classes.

Examples: Turn to page 5.
          Listen carefully.
          Don't forget to turn in your papers today.

1. _____

2. _____

3. _____

4. _____

5. _____

6. _____

2. Practice with pronouns.

Subject Pronouns	Object Pronouns
I	me
you	you
he	him
she	her
it	it
we	us
you (plural)	you (plural)
they	them

Subject pronouns identify the subject of a sentence.
Object pronouns identify the object of a verb.

Examples: *He* is my father.
I help *him* with his work.

She is my friend.
I like *her* very much.

They are my friends.
I help *them* learn English.

He needs a ride.
Take *him* with you.

Choose the correct form of the pronoun to complete the sentence.
  a. (He/Him) is my father.
  b. (He/Him) and I live in the same country.
  c. Give (I/me) the book, please.
  d. He is helping John and (I/me).
  e. His father asks (he/him) to drive.
  f. (They/Them) and their friends will be here.
  g. (We/Us) students need to study more.
  h. My friend and (me/I) are the same age.
  i. Can you help (we/us) with this?
  j. She helps John and (me/I).

    k. Do you know where (she/her) lives?

    l. (We/Us) boys are the only ones in the class from Saudi Arabia.

    m. Jim and (I/me) study together.

    n. We would like to meet (they/them).

    o. Would you like to meet (she/her), too?

    p. (She/Her) and I are friends.

    q. Please help Jane and (me/I).

3. Practice with verbs. Write the correct form of the verb. (Look for indications of verb tense, for example.)

    a. He _____ his father's car to San'a yes-
                      (drive)
    terday.

    b. When he goes to the city, he always _____
                                        (drive)
    his father's car.

    c. Ali was _____ the car when I saw him.
                    (drive)

    d. His father said to him, "_____care-
                             (drive)
    fully."

    e. They _____ with Jasem's uncle an
                 (eat)
    hour ago.

    f. When he visits his uncle, he usually _____
                                     (eat)
    with him.

    g. "_____ enough," they said to him.
                  (eat)

    h. "_____ sure to eat enough," they said.
                  (be)

    i. When he stopped, the man _____
                                    (get)
    into the car.

    j. Are you _____ him?
                  (help)

k. I think he was _____ in the desert
(walk)
when Ali saw him.

l. Did they _____ his uncle's place?
(find)

m. After they drove a long time, they _____
(find)
it.

n. "_____ the right place on your page,
(find)
please."

o. When he visits the city, he usually _____
(come)
to our house.

p. Did the girls _____ to class yesterday?
(come)

q. "_____ right here, please!" he shouted.
(turn)

r. "_____ to class regularly," said the
(come)
teacher.

s. When he came to the corner, he _____
(turn)
right.

t. When he comes to the corner, he _____
(turn)
right.

u. Will he _____ that way again?
(go)

v. Does he always _____ that way?
(go)

D. Questions for discussion.

1. Why did Ali feel like a *man* when his father asked him to drive to San'a for him? What kind of experience made you feel like a *man* (or *woman*) when you were a teenager?

2. Why do you think Ali *hesitated*, rather than stop immediately, when he saw Jasem on the road?
3. Do you think there was a reason, *other than that the road was rough*, why Ali did not want to continue on the road through the desert? Explain.
4. What do you think Jasem had in mind when he told Ali that *he would be sorry* if he took the other road?
5. What do you think happened to Jasem?

E.   Writing practice or more discussion.

1. Write a paragraph (or tell the class) about what kind of relationship you think Ali and his father had.
2. Write a paragraph (or tell the class) about an *interesting, humorous,* or *frightening* experience you had when visiting a foreign country.
3. Write a paragraph (or tell the class) about what you think really happened to Jasem. (Explain also *who* you think Jasem was.)
4. Write a paragraph (or tell the class) about what you think happened after this story ends.

F.   A bit of humor.

The Whole Truth

A rather shy seventeen-year-old high school boy was in the witness box in court to testify in an accident case.

When the attorney noticed that the young man was very nervous, he started out with a few off-the-subject questions to try to calm him down.

"I understand you play football," the attorney began.

"Yes, sir."

"What position do you play?"

"Quarterback, sir."

"And, are you a *good* quarterback?"

"Yes, sir, I am. Better than Johnny Logan, sir, but the coach doesn't seem to know that. He always plays Johnny before me."

The boy's parents, who were in the courtroom, were very surprised at what he said. When they asked him about it later he said, "You have to remember, mom and dad, that I was under oath!"

Overcorrection

In that same high school there was an English teacher who liked to have the students give suggestions for correcting each other's themes.

"Listen to what Ginny wrote in her theme," she said one day, with a paper in her hand, "'I ain't had no fun since my boyfriend, Alvin, moved away.' Now," continued the teacher, "how would you suggest Ginny correct that, George?"

"Well, she could forget about Alvin and go out with me."

Snowstorm

*Based on an incident told by a student from Tucson, Arizona.**

Norman Holton pushed the gear shift into *park* and sat back.

"It's no use, Maybelle," he said with a sigh. "I've tried everything I know, and we've only gotten into the snow deeper."

"Get us off this mountain, Norman!" his wife demanded. "The storm
5 hasn't let up a bit, and it's getting darker by the minute!"

Norman threw up his hands. "I *know* the storm has gotten worse!" he shouted at her. "And I know it's getting darker. But I also know that we have gone as far as we can go."

"You don't have to yell at me, you know," she snapped back. Then
10 she pulled up the collar of her coat, jammed her hands into her pockets, and slid over on the front seat till she was leaning against the door.

They sat in silence for a minute, while the snow swirled around the car. Then Maybelle broke the silence. "Why don't you carry a bag of sand in the car? That's what my father always did back in Minnesota."

15 "That's what my father did back in Minnesota," he imitated sarcastically.

"Don't make fun of my father!" she snapped.

"I'm not making fun of your father. But I've heard you say that so often, it rings in my ears: 'That's what my father always did back in
20 Minnesota.'" He shook his head again and forced out a little laugh.

---

*The elevation, above sea level, in Tucson, Arizona, is 2,600 feet (approximately 800 meters). In the Catalina Mountains, less than a two-hour drive from Tucson, there are roads with elevations of nearly 8,000 feet (almost 2,500 meters).

She looked at him around the collar of her coat. If looks could kill, Norman would have fallen dead over the steering wheel.

He looked at her out of the corner of his eye. "Now I suppose you're mad."

"Mad?" she muttered. "No, I'm furious!"

"Why?" he laughed, almost with a look of satisfaction.

"Because, in my opinion, this trip was unnecessary."

"What do you mean?" he asked, as his smile changed to a frown.

"Well, you're the one who wanted to go to the mountains to cut a Christmas tree. I said, 'Go buy one.' Remember? Now here we are, forty miles from sunny Tucson, in a *snowstorm,* of all things!" 30

Norman's mood changed again when Maybelle mentioned their reason for making this trip to the mountains from their home in Tucson, in the desert valley below. Yesterday he thought this could be a happy occasion. He should have known better. He hung his head as he spoke. 35 "The permit was only a dollar. But—but it wasn't so much the money. Somehow, I—I thought it sounded like fun to cut our own Christmas tree. And we certainly haven't had much fun together recently." He continued to look down as he waited for her response.

"Some fun!" she laughed. "Listen to that wind, Norman, and look at 40 that snow! Do you call this fun?"

Tears came to Norman's eyes. He pulled up the collar of his jacket and turned his head toward the side window of the car, acting as though he were trying to look out. With a lump in his throat, he opened the door of the car and stepped out. 45

"Where are you going?" demanded Maybelle.

"Nowhere," he answered in a hoarse whisper as he closed the car door.

"You haven't gone anywhere in the twenty years we've been married," she mumbled under her breath, but he didn't hear her. 50

The snow blew mercilessly against Norman's face until he turned away from the wind. He pulled up his collar, put his hands in his pockets, and leaned against the car. He tried to think of what he could do. It was bad enough to be in a situation like this, but it was always more difficult for him when Maybelle was along. In frustration, he hit 55 his fists together. Then, realizing that he had to do something, Norman tried to look down the road in both directions. He saw almost nothing, however. He couldn't even see the edge of the cliff, but he knew it was very near where the car stood, stuck in the snow. He finally decided to get back into the car. 60

As he sat behind the wheel again, he took off his gloves and rubbed his hands together.

"Have you decided what to do, Norman?" she asked in a sarcastic tone of voice.

65 "Well, I—I thought maybe . . ." he started slowly.

"Have you thought of going for help?" she interrupted. "Or aren't you man enough to venture out in a little wind and snow?"

"*Man* enough?" he said in a raised voice. "You mean *crazy* enough!"

"No, I mean *man* enough. You don't like it when I mention what my
70 father would do, but my dear father . . ."

"Let's leave your dear, *perfect* father out of this right now, okay?" he shouted.

Maybelle pulled her head down into the collar of her coat like a turtle retreating into its shell while Norman grabbed the steering wheel as
75 though he wanted to tear it off and throw it away. The breath from his nostrils came out into the cold air like the snorting breath of an angry bull.

Finally he turned toward her, with one elbow on the steering wheel and the other on the back of the seat. "Do you *really* want me to go out
80 there in that blizzard?" he asked.

"Why not?" she mumbled from inside her coat collar. "I haven't heard any better suggestion from the only other person here."

"Well, I happen to think it's safer for us to wait for someone to come along."

85 "Who's going to come along here, Norman?" she laughed, still not moving her head.

"Someone who has chains or a four-wheel-drive vehicle. That's who."

Still without turning to face him, she asked in a soft, but accusing
90 voice, "Why don't *we* have chains, Norman?"

"Now, blame me for that!" he said, throwing up his hands. "What next? For your information, we don't have chains because we live in sunny Tucson, Arizona. Remember?"

"Don't yell." she mumbled. "I'm not deaf, you know."

95 "I'm *not* yelling!" he shouted.

Just then, someone tapped on the window of the car. As Norman rolled down the window, a middle-aged man bent down and looked in. He wore only a light jacket and had nothing on his head. There was snow in his hair and frost on his small mustache. He smiled as he spoke
100 in a soft but clear voice.

"If you folks want to live through the night," he said, "dig yourselves into a snowbank. There's a big enough one over the ditch back there, just a little way behind your car."

Norman and Maybelle sat there, too surprised to say anything. The man smiled at them sympathetically and added, "Just dig yourselves in and huddle together. Believe me, it will save your lives. The storm will probably be over by daybreak." 105

Before either of them could say a word, the man turned, and they saw him no more. Norman got out of the car quickly and looked in the direction he thought he saw the man go, but he saw no one. He called, but there was no answer. Then he got back into the car. 110

"Who do you suppose that was?" asked Maybelle.

"I wish I knew," answered Norman. "Did you see what he had on? Only a light jacket? No hat? I don't even think he had gloves on, the way he kept his hands in his pockets." 115

"Did you see a vehicle anywhere?"

"No, and I didn't hear one either."

They sat there for a minute, not knowing what to say or think. Then Maybelle spoke: "What do you think about what he said?"

"I was just recalling something I've read about that," replied Norman. "The article, I remember, told about how the Eskimos in Canada and Alaska have always kept from freezing by taking shelter in the snow. And I have heard that in those igloos the Eskimos used to live in, the temperature was never much below freezing, no matter how cold it was outside." 125

"So, you think it's worth a try?"

"I suppose so. What do we have to lose? Also, we have warm clothes and this blanket we've been using as a seatcover in the car."

Norman and Maybelle Holton went out into the storm and, in a few minutes, found the place the man was talking about. They cut through the hard surface of the snow with their gloved hands, dug a hole large enough for the two of them, and climbed in. 130

Huddled in each other's arms, they felt warmer but shivered from fear. As the fierce wind howled outside their shelter, both of them vowed to themselves that if they lived through this, they were going to change some things in their lives. Neither one of them said anything about those thoughts, however. Then, finally, for the first time in years, they fell asleep holding each other close. 135

At daybreak they dug themselves out and found that the storm was over. They felt cold, but noticed that their fingers and toes were not numb. Then they looked and saw that two forest rangers were standing by their car. 140

"Oh, there you are," said one of the rangers, as he saw Norman and Maybelle walk toward them. "We've been looking for you. This *is* your
145 car, isn't it?"

"Yes, it is," said Norman.

"How did you know that the snow gives better protection than your car?" asked the other ranger.

"Well, a man came by and told us," replied Maybelle, "and we . . ."
150 "What man?" asked the ranger.

"A man about my age," said Norman. "Dark hair, mustache. And believe it or not, he was out in that storm with only a light jacket on. No hat. I don't even think he had gloves on."

"Did you talk to him?" asked the ranger.
155 "We wanted to, but he spoke to us and took off."

The rangers looked at each other. Then one of them said, "It looks like Mr. Porter has made another visit."

"Who's Mr. Porter?" asked Maybelle.

"Well," replied the ranger, "about five years ago, a man by the name
160 of Porter came up here with his wife and eight-year-old son, to get a Christmas tree. I guess you folks did the same. On the way back, the car got stuck in the snow, just about right here."

"Since then," the other ranger continued, "he has returned several times to tell people how to survive in a snowstorm."
165 "Why doesn't he dress for the winter weather up here?" asked Norman. The rangers looked at each other again and smiled.

"I guess you could say he doesn't have to, now," one of them answered.

"What do you mean?" asked Maybelle.
170 "Well," the ranger went on, "the Porter boy, who lived through the ordeal, told us what happened. He said his parents argued about what to do when they couldn't go on. Mr. Porter apparently became quite angry. The kid said his dad got out of the car and slammed the door, apparently going for help."
175 "During the night," continued the other ranger, "Mrs. Porter froze to death in the car, but the kid somehow made it. I guess he had a blanket around him."

"What about Mr. Porter?" Norman asked.

"Mr. Porter apparently couldn't see in the blowing snow when he left
180 the car. He walked off the cliff right about over there," he answered, pointing to a rocky ledge nearby. "He must have fallen at least 250 feet, almost straight down," continued the ranger. "We found him the next morning—dead."

A. Questions on the content of the story.

1. Where does this story take place?
2. What are the names of the two main characters?
3. Where did they live at the time of the story?
4. Why did they make this trip?
5. What did Maybelle say that her father carried in the car for emergencies like this?
6. How far from Tucson was this place in the mountains?
7. How much did they pay for the permit to cut a Christmas tree?
8. What did Maybelle think Norman should be *man enough* to do?
9. What did Norman think they should do?
10. Describe the man who tapped on their car window.
11. What did the man tell Norman and Maybelle to do?
12. Why did Norman and Maybelle decide to take his suggestion?
13. When did they come out of their shelter?
14. Who told them the story about the Porter family?
15. What did the rangers say happened to each of the three Porters—the father, the mother, and the eight-year-old boy?

B. Vocabulary practice.

1. Underline the correct meaning.
   a. When Maybelle said, "The storm hasn't *let up* a bit," she meant that (the storm was not getting any better/the snow was blowing mercilessly/it was getting darker).
   b. *Yell* means about the same as (imitate/snap/shout).
   c. When Maybelle said to her husband, "Don't *make fun of* my father!" she meant that she did not want her husband to (imitate/ridicule/have a good time with) her father.
   d. When Maybelle said she was *furious,* she meant (she was very angry/she wanted to be home in Tucson/she blamed Norman for getting stuck in the snow).
   e. Norman's *mood* changed when Maybelle mentioned their reason for making this trip. This means that (he hung his head/his feeling became different/cutting a tree sounded like fun).
   f. When Maybelle *mumbled under her breath,* (she spoke in a low voice/she spoke without breathing/she spoke slowly).
   g. Someone *tapped* on the window of the car, which means

that someone (knocked hard/knocked lightly/wanted to help them).

h. Norman said the man *took off* before they could speak to him, which means that he (walked into the storm/disappeared/went away quickly).

i. They *huddled* in each others arms, which means that (they felt warmer/they shivered from fear/they held each other close).

k. The rangers said that Mr. Porter told people how to *survive* in a snowstorm, which means that he told them how to (stay alive/keep warm/hold each other close).

l. The Porter boy *lived through the ordeal*, which means that he (survived a painful experience/had a blanket to keep him warm/lived to tell the story).

2. In the following sentences, change *no* to *not any*. (*Do not* change the tense of the verb.)

Examples: I see nothing.
I don't see anything.

I saw nothing.
I didn't see anything.

I have seen nothing.
I haven't seen anything.

a. Norman goes nowhere.

Norman _____.

b. He went nowhere.

He _____.

c. Norman has gone nowhere.

Norman _____.

d. Does no one see us?

_____ see us?

e. Did no one see us?

_____ see us?

f. Has no one seen us?

_____ seen us?

g. They say nothing to each other.

They _____ to each other.

h. They said nothing to each other.

They _____ to each other.

i. They have said nothing to each other.

They _____ to each other.

j. They get no help.

They _____ help.

k. They got no help.

They _____ help.

l. They have gotten no help.

They _____ help.

3. Change *not any* to *no.* (Do not change the tense of the verb.)

Examples: I don't have any money.
I have no money.
I didn't have any money.
I had no money.
I haven't had any money.
I have had no money.

a. She doesn't see anyone.

She _____.

b. She didn't see anyone.

She _____.

c. She hasn't seen anyone.

She _____.

d. I don't want anything.

I _____.

e. I didn't want anything.

I _____.

f. I haven't wanted anything.

I _____.

g. We don't go anywhere.

We _____.

h. We didn't go anywhere.

We _____.

  i. We haven't gone anywhere.

  We _____.
  j. I don't see anybody at all.

  I _____ at all.
  k. I didn't see anybody at all.

  I _____ at all.
  l. I haven't seen anybody at all.

  I _____ at all.
4. Match the *opposites*.

  a. nearby   **1.** warm
  b. numb   **2.** far away
  c. cool   **3.** down
  d. dead   **4.** alive
  e. better   **5.** full of feeling
  f. below   **6.** worse
                         7. above

C. Grammar practice.

Choose the correct form of the verb. Look carefully in the sentence for indications of which verb form you need.

Examples: The Holtons (go/<u>*went*</u>/gone) to the mountains together last week.
They have (go/went/<u>*gone*</u>) to the mountains many times.
They did not (<u>*go*</u>/went/gone) last year.

1. Maybelle opened her mouth and (speak/spoke/spoken) to him.
2. They have (go/went/gone) as far as they can go.
3. Norman has (hear/heard) her talk about her father too many times.
4. Yesterday Norman (think/thought) this would be fun.
5. He should have (know/knew/known) this would happen.
6. When he went out, the wind (blow/blew/blown) in his face.
7. Norman turned and (speak/spoke/spoken) to her.
8. I think Mr. Porter has (tap/tapped) on many car windows.
9. After Mr. Porter speaks to people, he always (takes off/took off/taken off) right away.

10. The Holtons left the car and (dig/dug) themselves into the snow.
11. "A number of people have (fall/fell/fallen) off this cliff," he said.
12. "Did the boy (survive/survived)?" he asked.
13. Five years ago, the boy (tell/told) the rangers what happened.
14. Mr. Porter (wears/wore/worn) the same jacket every time he comes.
15. The rangers have (came/come) to help.

D. Questions for discussion (in small groups, if possible).

1. Do you think Norman and Maybelle Holton were *on their way to* the mountains or *on their way home* when they ran into the snowstorm? Explain.
2. Why would people carry *sand* in the car for emergencies like this?
3. Why didn't Norman like to hear Maybelle talk about her father?
4. Why did *Norman's mood change* when Maybelle mentioned their reason for making this trip?
5. What happened to Norman's mood when Maybelle responded by laughing and saying, "Some fun! Listen to the wind, Norman, and look at that snow! Do you call this fun?"
6. When tears came to Norman's eyes, why did he turn his head toward the window of the car?
7. Why did Maybelle add "or aren't you man enough?" when she asked if he thought of going for help?
8. Why did Norman speak in a raised voice when he disagreed with Maybelle's suggestion that he go for help?
9. Why do you think Maybelle brought her father into the discussion again?
10. Why do you suppose Norman called Maybelle's father *perfect?*
11. What was Norman implying when he said, "we don't have chains because we live in sunny Tucson, Arizona?"
12. Why were the Holtons so surprised to see the man who came and spoke to them?
13. It seems that Maybelle Holton possibly lived at one time in Minnesota, yet she didn't seem to know anything about taking shelter in the snow. Why do you suppose that may have been?

14. Describe how you think Maybelle and Norman may have reacted when the rangers told them about Mr. Porter.

E. More discussion or writing practice.

1. Describe what you think Norman and Maybelle's relationship was like.
2. What indications are there that their marriage was perhaps in trouble before this happened?
3. When they were huddled together in the snow, both of them vowed to themselves that if they lived through this, they were going to change some things in their lives. Why do you suppose neither of them *said* anything to the other about that, however?
4. Do you think their relationship changed after this experience? Explain.
5. Tell the class what you think Maybelle told a good friend of hers about this experience when she returned to Tucson. Or write what you think Maybelle told her mother in a letter about this experience.

F. A bit of humor.
There are many stories about difficult people, both men and women. Let's smile a little over a story of each.

1. After he lost his eyesight, the English poet, John Milton, married a woman who became quite difficult to live with. A friend once said to the blind poet, "It's unfortunate that your wife is such a contrary person. She *looks* like a rose."

    "I'm sure she *is* a rose," replied Milton, who had never seen his wife, "for I feel the thorns every time I am close to her."

2. Quakers are peace-loving people who are usually mild-mannered. There was a Quaker, however, in Pennsylvania some years ago who was a very mean man. His neighbors said they never heard him speak a kind word.

    When he died, his neighbors all gathered around his grave. Then, as was the Quaker custom, everyone stood there in silence until someone felt that he had something to say.

    After many minutes of silence, one of the man's neighbors cleared his throat and said, "I'll say this for our departed neighbor here: There were some times when he was less mean than he was most of the time."

The Hanging Tree

Based on a story told by Mahdi Ahmed of Khartoum, Sudan.

I walked down the dusty main street of the village. Somehow it didn't look quite the same as I had remembered. But then, thirty years can change pictures in the mind which have been put there by a twelve-year-old boy.

5   In the middle of the village I found a shopkeeper who had been a friend of my father's. He was nearly eighty years old, but his actions were those of a much younger man. And his eyes were bright, even though the nearly coal-black skin of his face had become deeply wrinkled over the years.

10   He welcomed me warmly, embracing me for some time. Then he invited me to sit and talk with him. After I accepted his invitation, we sat down on two stools in the street in front of his shop.

"So, why have you come back here, Mahdi?" the old man asked as he looked me over. "You and your parents left here so long ago."

15   "Why does anyone return to the place of his youth?" I replied, wondering for a moment why he had asked. "I have wanted, for a long time, to walk some of the old pathways again. So here I am, in the village where I grew up."

At that moment I did not feel that I could tell this man that I was one

20 of the chief investigators for the secret service and that I had come here on a very special mission. My mission was to find the man who had assassinated an important government official three years before. Everyone knew that the person responsible for that mysterious murder

had not yet been found. What very few people were aware of, however, was that I was the one who had the responsibility to investigate this case. 25

For nearly three years our investigation had done little more than wear out shoes and vehicles as we searched for the assassin from one part of northeast Africa to another. Then, suddenly, all leads pointed to this area in the Kassala Province of my country, Sudan, where the assassination had taken place. Because I had grown up here, I decided to come myself to investigate, rather than send someone else. 30

"I don't suppose there are many people left here in the village that I knew when I was a child," I said, trying to make conversation with the old man. 35

"No, I don't think so," he replied, as he leaned forward on his stool with both hands on his old wooden cane. "Thirty years is a long time, Mahdi. Things change." He stared off in the distance, squinting his eyes for a clearer look into the past. Then he said almost in a whisper, "So *many* things change." 40

"They certainly do," I agreed, trying to keep up the conversation, while my thoughts were on the real purpose of my mission.

The old man then turned and pointed down the wide, dusty street to the edge of the village. "Many people left here when they closed the old prison, you know, about ten years after your family left here." 45

I looked in the direction he was pointing and saw that nothing more remained of the prison than the partly crumbled walls.

"By the way," I asked, "whatever happened to the *hanging tree* that stood in front of the prison? I don't see it there."

He shook his head as he said with a frown, "Do you mean *the tree of* 50 *moans and groans?*"

"Yes. You know, when I was a child, I believed what people said about that tree."

The old man stamped his cane several times. Then he spoke in a raised voice with a look of disgust on his wrinkled face. "Hysterical 55 people told those stories!" Then he turned to me. "Can you believe that mature adults could let their imaginations run away like that? 'The ghosts of dead men live in that tree,' they always said, 'You can hear them moan and groan when you pass there at night.' Such nonsense!"

"I remember a friend of my mother's who said she even heard the 60 rattle of chains when she passed there at night," I said with a smile.

Again he stamped his cane in disgust. "Foolish, ignorant people they were, I tell you! Mostly women."

"But men *did die* there, didn't they?" I asked. "I remember . . ."

65   "Oh yes, indeed!" he interrupted. "Many men died there. In those days they executed criminals in public by hanging them in that tree. They hanged them at daybreak. Then the bodies hung there all day, until sundown, with the chains still on their feet."

"I guess my father and mother never let me see that. It must have
70   been a gruesome sight."

"It was. Yes, it was. But what people *imagined* when they passed there at night was just as bad. It was so ridiculous!"

"Whatever happened to the tree?" I asked.

"It died years ago, but that didn't stop people from hearing strange
75   things there at night. I think some of the stories got worse!" he said as he hit the ground with his cane again.

"What happened to the tree?" I asked again.

"Just two or three weeks ago, they cut it down and told the people they could use it for firewood." Then he laughed. "But these silly peo-
80   ple won't touch that wood. They would rather eat raw food than build fires with that wood. The only ones who have used any of it have been wanderers who have passed through here. They use it because they don't know where the wood comes from."

"Wanderers?" I asked. "Have you seen any recently?" The man we
85   were looking for, according to reports, had recently disguised himself as a wanderer.

"Yes, there was a strange one here this morning. Wouldn't talk to anyone. I watched him carefully when he went out of my store. Just before he left the village, he tied together a bundle of sticks from that
90   hanging tree, put it over his shoulder, and headed for the hills."

"Which way did he go?"

"That way," he said, pointing north. "Why?"

"Oh, I just was wondering. It's a hobby of mine to talk to wanderers. I think they're interesting."

95   "Well, be careful, if you talk to that one. He seemed really strange."

"How old do you think he was?"

"He looked quite old," he answered. "But you never know about those men. They've usually led a hard life."

The man I was looking for was not old, not more than forty. But for
100   various reasons I decided I wanted to talk to this strange one.

I stayed with that shopkeeper and his wife that night. Then the next morning I set out for the hills, trying to look like no more than an ordinary traveler. By asking here and there and using a few of my professional skills, I found the wanderer before nightfall. He was kneeling at the mouth of a cave, staring into space. Beside him was what appeared to be a part of the bundle of sticks he took from the hanging tree. His wrinkled brow indicated that he was much older than the man I was looking for, but still I approached him with caution.

I spoke to him in Arabic, but it seemed that he didn't hear me. Then, I tried to get a response by using what little I knew of several Sudanese tribal languages. He still continued to kneel there, staring straight ahead, as though in a trance.

Again, I spoke in Arabic. When I asked about other wanderers he showed a little nervousness. Then I told him who I was and showed him my identification. Suddenly, he fell to the ground face down with his arms outstretched.

With one hand on the pistol I had in a shoulder strap under my robe, I rolled him over and loosened his worn garment.

In a few seconds he opened his eyes. He was in a cold sweat. As he opened his mouth and began to speak, tears began to roll from his eyes.

"I will go with you quietly," he muttered. "Please don't harm me!"

I was almost too surprised to speak, but I jumped back and instinctively aimed my pistol at him.

"It is good that you have found me," he wept. "God has aged me thirty years in these three."

I continued to take precautions, although it appeared that I was dealing with a man who was more defeated than dangerous.

The man continued to lie on his back with his arms outstretched. He had a terrible look of anguish on his face. Then he cried so hard that his whole body shook.

"How hard God is on those who run with the weight of guilt on their heads!" he wept.

"What do you mean?" I asked, almost sympathetically.

"Many times, in these years of running," he sobbed, "I have heard the moans and groans of a dying man in my dreams at night. And now," he wept, "and now, God has spoken to me through fire in broad daylight."

"Through fire?" I asked in surprise. "God has communicated with you through fire?"

"Yes, through fire!" he sobbed in a pathetic whisper. "Today when I made a fire from these sticks, I heard the moans and groans of a dying man come *out of the fire*." He closed his eyes and shook as he cried.

"Then, as I looked into the flames," he went on, "God even rattled
145 chains in front of me in that fire—chains which should be on *my* feet."

A. Questions on the content of the story.

1. How long had it been since Mahdi left this village?
2. How old was he when he left? How old was Mahdi when this story took place?
3. Why did Mahdi come back to the village?
4. When he was talking with the shopkeeper, what did he say his reason was for returning to the village?
5. Why didn't he tell the old man what his mission was?
6. At the time of this story, how long had they looked for the assassin?
7. When all leads in the investigation pointed to the area of this village, why did this chief investigator come *himself*, rather than send someone else?
8. Find Sudan on a map of Africa. What are some of the neighboring countries in northeast Africa, where they may have searched for the assassin?
9. How long before this story took place had they closed the prison in the village?
10. How much of the prison still stood?
11. What had some of the village people said about the hanging tree?
12. Did the old man believe the stories? How do you know?
13. Why didn't the village people use the wood from the hanging tree for firewood?
14. Who did use some of it?
15. Why did Mahdi ask the old man if he had seen any wanderers recently?
16. Why did the investigator think that this strange wanderer was *not* the man he was looking for?
17. Why did he decide to try to find him?
18. What did the wanderer have next to him when the investigator found him?
19. Where did the investigator carry a pistol?
20. What did the wanderer say he heard in the fire which had been made from the sticks from the hanging tree?

B. Vocabulary practice.

 1. Choose the correct answer.
  a. Mahdi said he wanted to *walk some of the old pathways again*, which means that (he enjoyed traveling/he wanted to see the place where he grew up/he wanted to find an assassin).
  b. The investigator was on a special *mission*, which means (he had a special job to do/he was a missionary/he was an investigator).
  c. All *leads in the investigation pointed to this area*, which means that (he decided to go himself/it was in the Kassala Province/there were indications that the assassin may be here).
  d. *Nothing more remained* of the prison than the partly crumbled walls. This means that (it was all that was still there/they no longer used the prison/the walls had fallen).
  e. The old man called what the people said about the tree *nonsense*, which means that (he thought it was sensible/he didn't hear it himself/he thought it was not sensible).
  f. Mahdi said it must have been a *gruesome sight* to see a body hang in that tree all day with chains still on its feet. This means that (people heard moans and groans there/ people saw it/it was a terrible thing to see).
  g. The investigator said that the assassin had *disguised himself as a wanderer*, which means that (he made himself look like a wanderer/he was a guide for wanderers/he was strange).
  h. Mahdi said that it was a *hobby* of his to talk to wanderers. This means that he talked to wanderers (for the purpose of investigating them/for his personal enjoyment/because they were interesting).
  i. The wanderer was kneeling at *the mouth of a cave* when he found him. This means that the wanderer was kneeling (staring into space/in a cave/at the opening of a cave).
  j. It seemed as though the wanderer was *in a trance*, which means that (he did not seem to hear or see anything/he was in an entrance/he was really strange).
  k. The wanderer said that God is *hard* on those who run with the weight of guilt on their heads. This means that (it is

difficult to run when you are guilty/God is severe with a guilty person/it is not easy to run away from God).

2. Match the words with more or less the *same* meanings.

a. harm	**1.** communicate
b. aim	**2.** discover
c. weep	**3.** go back
d. find	**4.** hurt
e. speak	**5.** point
f. return	**6.** cry
g. leave	**7.** go away
	8. groan

3. Match the *opposites*.

a. old	**1.** after
b. black	**2.** calm
c. before	**3.** narrow
d. wide	**4.** strange
e. hysterical	**5.** white
f. foolish	**6.** pleasant
g. gruesome	**7.** wise
	8. young

4. When the word *hang* means to execute by hanging or to commit suicide by hanging, the past tense is *hanged*. For other meanings of *hang*, the past tense is *hung*.
Choose the correct past tense.
   a. We (hung/hanged) a picture on the wall.
   b. The troubled man (hung/hanged) himself.
   c. They (hung/hanged) the criminal at daybreak.
   d. The rope (hung/hanged) down from the tree.
   e. The chains (hung/hanged) from the feet of the murderer.
   f. The criminal's body (hung/hanged) there all day.
   g. I (hung/hanged) my coat in the closet.

C. Discussion or writing practice.

(For discussion, divide into small groups if possible.)

   1. The story indicates that the years can change things we remembered as children. Tell about how *you* found, after a number of years, that something (or someone) was different from what you remembered as a child.

2. The old shopkeeper says that things *do* actually change through the years. What do you think may have changed the most in this village in the thirty years since Mahdi and his family left? Explain.
3. Why do you suppose many people left this village after the prison was closed?
4. Why do you think they executed criminals *in public*?
5. Does the government execute criminals in public in your country?
6. What do you suppose was the real reason people heard moans and groans from the hanging tree at night? Explain.
7. There is the belief in many cultures that the spirits or souls of people who died violently remain in the area where they died. Explain what you have heard about this belief, giving examples.
8. Do you think this old man used any of the wood from the hanging tree for firewood himself? Explain why it may have been a good idea for him to do so.
9. What do you think were some of the *professional skills* this investigator used to find the wanderer? Explain.
10. Why do you suppose this man wept when he confessed to the assassination? Explain.
11. Make up a dialogue between Mahdi and the shopkeeper which may have taken place later. (If this is done *orally*, two people can *act* the parts).

D. A bit of interesting information.

In Tombstone, Arizona, they tell a story, which they say is true, about something that happened there in the 1880s, when they hanged criminals in public.

They say that one day, when there was going to be an execution, a large crowd gathered to watch. In fact, the crowd was so big that the guards could not get near the execution platform and scaffold with the wagon which held the prisoner. Suddenly the prisoner shouted from behind the bars in the prison wagon, "You don't need to push and shove, ladies and gentlemen! Nothing is going to happen until I get there!"

Tombstone, Arizona, which was one of the largest and wildest cities in the American West over one hundred years ago, is today a friendly and peaceful town of about 2,000.

Now every year thousands of tourists visit historic Tombstone, which still retains the flavor of the Old West. Among the interesting places people visit is Boothill Cemetery on the edge of town. There, the epitaphs on the tombstones tell something about what the town was like a hundred years ago. Do you understand what the message on this one means?

Going Fishing

Based on a story told by Khalil Al-Sahoti of Qatar.

Abdul walked slowly along the sandy road toward the gulf. He was heading for the place where he and his father frequently went fishing. He had never been fishing alone before, but he didn't feel a bit afraid. Why should he? After all, he had just passed his fourteenth birthday.
5 And he knew how to fish and where to go. Also, he knew where *not* to go.

It was important to know where *not* to go because there was a tribal village not far from the place where Abdul and his father usually went fishing. But he knew enough to stay away from there. Of course, he
10 sometimes wondered how many of the strange stories people told about the tribespeople were true, anyway.

With these thoughts running through his head as he walked, Abdul looked up and saw a little donkey standing by the side of the road. He clapped his hands, but the animal didn't move. He walked up to the
15 donkey and slapped it on the back, but it still didn't stir. "I think this dumb thing wants to take me fishing," Abdul said to himself. Then he got on its back, but still the animal stood like a statue.

Abdul then leaned forward and yelled into one of the ears of the donkey, "Let's go fishing, stupid!" With that, the animal began to run.
20 Abdul tried to control the donkey, but when he found that he could not, he just hung on.

Instead of taking Abdul where he wanted to go, however, the donkey took him over a little hill to an inlet on the gulf very near the village of the tribespeople. Abdul realized where he was and wanted to get out of

there fast, but the donkey wouldn't budge. Abdul got off and started to 25
run, but then he noticed that there were fish jumping in the waves near
the shore. He stopped and watched. Then he looked around. Since
there was no one there, he couldn't see any harm in staying for a little
while. And he thought it would be nice to take a few of those fish home.

As Abdul got his line ready and walked into the water, the little 30
donkey stood nearby and watched him. When Abdul caught nothing the
first few times he threw in his line, the donkey made sounds almost like
laughter. "Laugh while you can, stupid!" shouted Abdul. "When I ride
you back home, I'll kick you all the way!" Then he turned around and
threw his line in again. 35

All of a sudden there was a strong pull on the line. In a minute he had
the largest fish he had ever caught. The fish didn't even put up a fight.
In fact, it almost seemed to want the boy to put a rope through its mouth
and gill.

Abdul was so excited about the size of the fish that he decided to go 40
home with only this one. Still standing in the shallow water, he threw
the fish over his shoulder and held the rope tightly in front of him with
both hands. Then he looked for the donkey but couldn't see him anywhere around. As Abdul started to walk out of the water, he heard a
strange voice say, "It's no more than right that you carry me back, since 45
I carried you here."

"What?" cried the boy. "The fish is talking! Or am I hearing things?"

"You're hearing right. Now, please take me back to the roadside
where you found me."

Abdul felt fear in every part of his body. As his mouth opened wide in 50
surprise, so did his hands, and he dropped the fish. Just then, a knee-
deep wave came in from the sea. When Abdul looked down after the
wave washed back, all he saw on the wet sand was his rope; the fish was
gone.

Abdul ran home as fast as his legs would carry him, without looking 55
back once. When he arrived, he didn't say anything to anyone but just
sat behind the house with his head in his hands. "Why did I do it? Why
did I do it?" he kept on saying to himself. "I shouldn't have stayed
there."

Finally, his father approached him. "Son," he said, "you have said 60
nothing since you came home from fishing. Is it so bad to come home
with no fish? Tomorrow will be another day."

Then, with tears in his eyes, Abdul said, "Oh, father, I do not feel
bad because I came home without fish but because I did something I
shouldn't have done." 65

"And what was that?" asked the father.

"Instead of going to the place where we usually fish, I went to an inlet near the tribespeople's village, and . . ."

"An inlet? I know where that is! I should have warned you about that
70 place!"

"Why, father?"

"Because strange things happen there."

"What kind of strange things?" Abdul asked, saying nothing about what had happened to him.

75 "I have heard of many things," answered the father, "but let me tell you what happened to me there once."

"Tell me, father! Please tell me!" said the boy excitedly.

The father sat down and began his story. "One day, a few years ago, I was on the way to our usual fishing place. Along the road I saw a little
80 donkey standing like a statue."

"Did you ride him, father?" asked the boy.

"Yes, as a matter of fact, I did. The way he stood there, he almost seemed to ask me to ride him. Even when I got on his back, he didn't move. Then I slapped him, and he began to run. And that's where he
85 went."

"Where?"

"To that inlet near the tribespeople's village. Since I had no reins to control him, I had to let him go where he pleased, and that's where he went. I wanted to leave there, of course, but I couldn't get the donkey
90 to move. When I got off his back, I saw fish jumping in the waves, so I decided to stay. After all, there was no one there."

"What happened then?" asked the boy with great interest. "Did the donkey stand there and watch you fish?"

"No, he didn't. In fact, I never saw him again."

95 "You didn't?" said the boy with a look of surprise on his face.

"No, I didn't. But let me tell you the rest of the story."

"I'm sorry, father. Please go on."

"I had a spear with me that day, a very special spear which I had made myself. As soon as I walked carefully into the water, a large fish
100 came near me. I raised my spear and put it into the side of the fish and held onto the rope I had attached to the spear." As Abdul's father tried to go on, his voice cracked with emotion.

"Go on, father. Tell me what happened next!"

"As the fish rolled over," the father continued, "it let out an awful cry
105 of agony. It sounded like a dying *man*, but it was the fish! Then, two or three times more I heard that cry. In my surprise, I let go of the rope. Then the fish swam swiftly away with my spear in his side."

"What happened, after that?" asked the boy, becoming more excited by the minute.

"Well, nothing more happened that day," replied the father. "But 110 after that, I frequently heard that cry of agony in my sleep at night. It was like the cry of a man in pain after he had been hit in battle."

"That isn't the end of the story, is it?" asked the boy, almost unable to contain his excitement.

"No, that's not all," the father went on. "About a week later I had to 115 go to the village to talk to one of the men of the tribe. When I went to the man's home, there, hanging on the wall in that man's house, was my spear!"

"Are you sure it was the same one you had used, father?"

"Yes, my son, I am sure. As I told you, I had made the spear myself." 120

"Did you ask the man where he found it?"

"Yes, I did. And he only looked at me strangely and said nothing. About that same time, his wife asked me to have dinner with the family. I didn't want to offend them, so I said 'yes.' Then, when the tribesman and I went outside to wash, he removed his robe. There, to my surprise, 125 I saw an ugly wound in his side in the same place where I had put my spear into the fish."

"What are you trying to tell me, father?"

"I'm not sure what I'm trying to tell you, my son," answered the father, as he stared off into space, "but I left there as quickly as I could." 130

Abdul got up and took his father's hand. "Father," he said, "I have something to tell you."

A. Questions on the content of the story.

1. Where did this story take place?
2. How old was Abdul at the time?
3. Where was the donkey when Abdul saw him?
4. Why couldn't Abdul control the donkey when he was on his back?
5. Why was Abdul afraid when he arrived at the inlet?
6. Why did he decide to stay?
7. Why did Abdul become angry with the donkey?
8. Why did Abdul decide to go home after he had caught only one fish?
9. Who appeared to be speaking to Abdul?
10. What did Abdul do when he got home?
11. When did his father decide to tell Abdul what had happened to him at that inlet?

12. What was the difference in the two methods which the father and son used in fishing?
13. What kind of sound seemed to come from the fish into which the father had put the spear?
14. When did Abdul's father hear that same sound later?
15. Where did the father again see the spear which he had lost?
16. Why was the father so sure that the spear was his?
17. Why did the tribesman remove his robe?
18. Where, on the tribesman's body, was there a wound?

B. Vocabulary practice.

1. Choose the correct meaning.
   a. Abdul was *heading for* the place where he and his father frequently fished, which means that he was (going fishing alone/going in that direction/going to the gulf).
   b. The animal *stood like a statue*, which means that (it was not a real animal/it wanted to give Abdul a ride/it didn't move).
   c. *An inlet* is (a recess in a shoreline/a dangerous place on a beach/a place near a tribal village).
   d. The donkey wouldn't *budge*, which means that (he wouldn't move/he wouldn't run/he wouldn't let anyone control him).
   e. Abdul *couldn't see any harm* in staying, which means that (he didn't want to injure anyone/he didn't want anyone to injure him/he thought it was all right).
   f. Abdul's father let the donkey go *where he pleased*, which means that he let him (go to an inlet/go where he wanted to/go with no reins).
   g. Abdul's father heard an awful *cry of agony*, which means that (it sounded like someone was in pain/it sounded like a man/it sounded like the fish was dying).
   h. Abdul's father didn't want *to offend* the tribespeople, which means that (he didn't want to argue with them/he didn't want to insult them/he didn't want to eat with them).
   i. The man *removed his robe*, which means that (he took it off/he had to wash/he wanted to show the ugly wound).
   j. Abdul's father *stared off into* space as he spoke, which means (he looked at the sky/he looked blankly/he was afraid).

2. Match those words which mean approximately the *same*.

a. little	**1.** not far
b. near	**2.** not deep
c. strange	**3.** powerful
d. strong	**4.** small
e. large	**5.** thin
f. shallow	**6.** big
g. awful	**7.** mysterious
	8. terrible

3. Match the *opposites*.

a. slowly	**1.** calmly
b. usually	**2.** loosely
c. excitedly	**3.** rarely
d. carefully	**4.** recklessly
e. swiftly	**5.** slowly
f. tightly	**6.** quickly
	7. ugly

C. Grammar practice.

1. Choose the correct form of the verb. Look for indications of *tense* in the sentences.

a. Abdul and his father have usually (went/gone) fishing together.

b. Yesterday Abdul (goes/went) fishing alone.

c. As the boy passed by, the donkey just (stands/stood) there.

d. He had always (wondering/wondered) if those stories were true.

e. After he spoke to the donkey it (began/begins) to run.

f. The donkey did not (go/went) where Abdul wanted.

g. He was (yelled/yelling) at him when I saw him.

h. Abdul had never (catch/caught) a fish that large before.

i. Had he ever (rode/ridden) on the back of an animal before?

j. He decided to go home after he (catch/caught) only one fish.

k. As he (stands/stood) there, he heard a strange voice.

l. "I have never (heard/hear) a fish talk!" he exclaimed.

m. He hadn't (stayed/staying) there long before he saw the fish.

n. His father had (saw/seen) some strange things in that village.

    o. Before they eat, they always (wash/washed).
    p. As he listened, his father (tells/told) him what happened.
    q. The boy had (became/become) very excited.
    r. Was that all that (happens/happened) while you were there?
    s. What has he (trying/tried) to tell his son?
    t. Abdul had not yet (tell/told) his story.

2. Finish the sentences. Use ideas from *your* life and experience. *Do not* use ideas from this story. (Be careful to use the correct form of the verb.)

    a. I have never _____.

    b. My father sometimes _____.

    c. Did the teacher _____?

    d. My friend and I haven't _____.

    e. When she talks, _____.

    f. Does your friend _____?

    g. He usually goes _____.

    h. Hasn't he ever _____?

    i. Have you _____?

    j. When I speak English, _____.

    k. Does the boy _____?

    l. Did we _____?

    m. They were standing _____.

    n. While they are working, _____.

    o. I've always wondered why _____.

D. Questions for discussion (in small groups, if possible).

1. Why do you think Abdul had never gone fishing alone before?
2. Do you think the donkey really laughed at Abdul, or was it his imagination? Explain.
3. Why did Abdul look for the donkey after he caught the fish?
4. Why did the father's voice crack with emotion when he spoke of spearing the fish?

5. Do you think Abdul's father ate with the tribesman's family before he left there? Explain.
6. Why do you think Abdul's father had not told him this story before?
7. Why did Abdul wait to hear his father's story before he decided to tell his own?

E. Writing practice (or more discussion).

1. Describe Abdul's feeling when he *felt fear in every part of his body.*
2. Tell (or write) about a time you had a feeling like that.
3. Describe how Abdul felt when he got home.
4. Explain what kind of relationship you think this father and son had.
5. Explain why you think it's good for a parent and child to be able to speak freely and frankly with each other. Give at least one example.

F. Storytelling and conversation (in groups of no more than four or five, if possible).

1. Play the part of Abdul, telling his story to his father. (Another member of the class can play the part of the father, interrupting with a few questions, like Abdul did when his father told his story.)
2. With another member of your group, make up a conversation between Abdul and his father—which takes place *after* Abdul tells his father his story—who discuss their experiences.
3. Tell your group a strange story like this which you may have heard in your part of the world.

G. A bit of humor.

One of the largest and finest delicatessens in New York advertizes
"Name your sandwich. If we don't have it, we'll get it for you!"
One man read the sign one day and decided to test their skill at getting what he wanted. He ordered a whale meat sandwich and a salad of greens from the intestines of the same whale.
The waiter returned to the man's table in a few minutes with this message: "I'm sorry sir, but the chef says that he will not kill one of his whales for just one sandwich and one salad."

One day two men rented a boat and rowed to the middle of a lake to go fishing. After they pulled in one fish after the other, one of them looked at the other and laughingly said, "I guess we should mark this place so we can come back here again tomorrow. Then he took a piece of chalk from his pocket and put an "X" on the side of the boat."

The other man looked at him and said, "You dummy! Tomorrow they probably won't even give us the same boat."

In the Operating Room

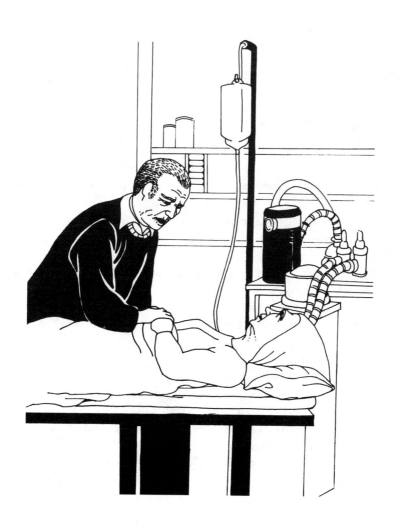

Based on an experience reported by Beth and Tom Mendel of Ottawa, Ontario, Canada.

Beth Mendel sat close to her husband on the front seat of their car as they drove down the highway toward the hospital. She knew by her husband's actions that he had another of his feelings—a feeling that something was going to happen. She knew, too, without looking, by
5 how he squeezed her hand, that he had tears in his eyes and a lump in his throat.

"What's the matter, Tom?" she asked, as she turned toward him to confirm her suspicions.

"Nothing, Beth, honey, nothing," he replied in a hoarse whisper. He
10 looked straight ahead toward the traffic on the road, cleared his throat, and added, "Why are you asking?"

"I know you too well, Tom," she said softly. "You have one of those feelings again that something is going to happen, don't you?"

Tom turned into the parking lot of the hospital and parked the car.
15 Then he turned to Beth and took her hand. "Beth, honey," he said with a sigh, as tears rolled down his cheeks, "I don't know what's wrong with me. I'm just a little nervous about your surgery, I guess."

"You shouldn't be," she replied, shaking her head. "The doctor said that this is not a serious operation. I'm going to be home again in three
20 days!"

"I know, honey, and I'm sure everything will be all right."

As the two walked hand-in-hand toward the front door of the hospital,

Beth added, "And you know, too, of course, that I will be in the hands of
the *One* who has *all things* in His hands."

"I know, honey. Please forgive me for acting silly."   25

As they entered the hospital and waited at the admissions desk, Beth
became a little apprehensive herself. After all, she had learned from
past experience that Tom's special feelings were never silly. She recalled how in their first year of marriage, thirty-seven years ago, he had
a strong feeling that something was going to happen to his father—the   30
day before he was killed in an accident. And there had been too many
other times when these feelings of Tom's were like prophecies.

After they finished filling out the admissions forms, they put Beth's
things in her room and went together to a nearby lounge to talk. Later,
when the hospital lights blinked to signal the end of visiting hours, Tom   35
turned to his wife and said, "I'm going to come in the morning before
your surgery. We can have prayer together, and . . ."

"Don't come that early," Beth interrupted. "They told me that I'll be
in the recovery room by eight o'clock. Why don't you come at that
time?"   40

"I'm going to come at 6:30, mom, before they take you to the operating room.

"But why?"

"I just want to be here," he said as tears again came to his eyes.

The lights blinked again, so he kissed her and left.   45

As he walked down the corridor on his way out of the hospital, Tom
wondered if he should have told Beth why he thought he should be in
the hospital while she was in surgery. "But," he said to himself, "she
would have laughed if I'd have told her that I have a strange feeling that
she is going to *need me* in the operating room." Smiling through his   50
tears as he walked toward the front door of the hospital, he said to
himself, "It even sounds crazy to me. What could she possibly need *me*
for in the operating room, anyway? I've never even been able to stand
the sight of blood. And what's an operation without a little blood?"

Meanwhile, Beth went to her room, where she decided to sit for a   55
little while with the lights off. The lights from the street below cast
shadows on the walls as she sat there in thought.

She smiled as she thought of her big, lovable husband. At sixty-two,
he was as big and masculine as he was when he played college football.
And yet, at times he was as sentimental as a sensitive child.   60

Beth thought, too, of how Tom had called her "mom" tonight. Like
many parents, they had called each other "mom" and "dad" while their

children were small. In recent years, however, Tom had not called her "mom" except under very special circumstances. After all, he liked the
65 sound of "Beth" and preferred to use it.

What Beth thought about more than anything else, as she sat in the semidarkness of her hospital room, was this feeling which she knew Tom had that something was going to happen at the time of her operation. He hadn't actually told her that he thought something was going to go
70 wrong, but she was sure that that's what it was. These feelings of his scared her sometimes. She thought, in fact, that he was becoming something of a psychic.

Tom did come early in the morning. And after the two of them had prayed and talked together for a few minutes, the nurses came to take
75 Beth to the surgical ward.

The last thing Tom said was, "I wish they'd let me go with you, mom!"

The nurses smiled as Beth replied, "Well, honey, at least you'll be there in spirit, won't you?"
80 Tom's eyes had tears so big he couldn't see, and he answered almost in a whisper, "Sure I will, mom! Sure I will!"

As they rolled her down the corridor, Beth wondered again about Tom's feeling, but smiled this time as she said to herself, "Maybe he's just getting more sentimental with age!"
85 Tom stood in the hallway until Beth was out of sight. Then he went to the hospital coffee shop where he ordered a cup of coffee and sat down at a table. He sat there for a number of minutes, sipping nervously, and stared at the sugar bowl in the middle of the table.

In the operating room, everything seemed ready, so the head sur-
90 geon told the anesthetist to begin.

"Just breathe as normally as you can, Mrs. Mendel," he said, as he began to administer the anesthetic.

For some reason, instead of breathing normally, Beth took a very deep breath and froze. In a second, her entire body seemed paralyzed.
95 The nurses and doctors worked frantically to get her to breathe, but nothing seemed to work. Beth could hear them shout orders to each other and could feel everything they did to her, but she was unable to breathe or move.

Suddenly she heard the footsteps of her husband. Then she saw him
100 stand over her, felt the touch of his hand, and heard him say, "Come on, mom, you can do it." Immediately, Beth relaxed and began breathing.

Since the anesthetic began to take effect and everything seemed to be all right, the surgeons decided to proceed with the operation.

About an hour later, in the recovery room, Beth opened her eyes and saw Tom at her bedside. Before either of them had said a word, howev- 105 er, the chief surgeon walked into the room. He stood by the bed and said, "I guess you know you gave us a little scare in the operating room, Mrs. Mendel."

"I know," she replied. "I don't know what happened. I could hear you, and I could feel when you touched me. I just couldn't breathe." 110 Then she smiled as she added, "It's a good thing you let Tom come in there. When he talked to me, for some reason everything was all right."

Tom Mendel and the surgeon looked at each other. Then the doctor said to Beth, "Your husband was *not* in the operating room, Mrs. Mendel, but it was a good thing you *thought* he was, if that's what helped." 115

"You mean he *wasn't* there?" she asked in surprise. "I even heard his footsteps. Do . . . do you mean I imagined all that?"

"I suppose so," smiled the doctor. "But your imagination was more effective than all our efforts to revive you."

Just then an orderly looked through the window in the door of the 120 recovery room. When he saw Tom Mendel, he opened the door and said, "There you are! Are you all right?"

"Am *I* all right?" asked Tom, looking quite surprised. "Of course, I'm all right. Why are you asking?"

"Well," said the orderly, "I saw you in the coffee shop, staring into 125 space with a cup of coffee in your hand about an hour ago. You looked like you were worried about something, so I walked over to your table and said, 'Are you okay, Mister?' That's when you got up, took my hand, and said something like, 'Come on, mom, you can do it.' Well, I thought you needed some help, so I ran to get a doctor. By the time I got back 130 there, you were gone." Then, when the orderly saw Tom laugh and shake his head, he asked, "Are you *sure* you're all right?"

A.   Questions on the content of the story.

   1. Where were Tom and Beth going when the story began?
   2. Why were they going there?
   3. What made Beth think her husband had a feeling that something was going to happen?
   4. How long had Beth and Tom Mendel been married?
   5. When did Beth become apprehensive? Why did she become apprehensive *at that time?*
   6. When did Tom and Beth go to the lounge to talk?

7. When did Tom tell Beth that he wanted to come back early in the morning?
8. Why didn't Beth want him to come?
9. When did Tom leave the hospital?
10. What was the strange feeling that Tom had?
11. Where did Beth decide to sit and think after Tom left?
12. What do we learn about Tom Mendel from his wife's thoughts?
13. How did Beth feel about her husband's strange feelings?
14. Where did Tom go after the nurses took Beth to the surgical ward?
15. What happened when the anesthetist administered the anesthetic?
16. When did Beth start breathing again?
17. Where did Tom and the chief surgeon talk with Beth after the operation?
18. Who else came into the recovery room?
19. Why did he come into the room when he saw Tom Mendel?
20. How had the orderly tried to help Tom when he saw him in the coffee shop?

B. Vocabulary practice.

1. Underline the correct answer.
   a. Beth thought that her husband had *a lump in his throat*, which means that she thought (he had swallowed something/ he was full of emotion/he had a strange feeling).
   b. When Beth turned toward her husband *to confirm her suspicions*, she expected (to see him act guilty/to see him look straight ahead/to see tears in his eyes).
   c. Beth said she would be *in the hands of the One who has all things in His hands*, which means that she felt (God would take care of her/her husband would take care of her/the surgeons would take care of her).
   d. Beth recalled that many of Tom's feelings were *like prophecies*, which means that (she realized that he acted silly/she knew his feelings were usually right/she was a little apprehensive).
   e. The thought of his being needed in the operating room seemed *crazy* to him, which means that (it didn't make sense to him/he thought something was wrong with him/he didn't like the sight of blood).

f. Beth thought her husband was *becoming something of a psychic,* which means that (his feelings scared her/she thought he had some kind of special power/her husband knew something was going to happen).

g. Beth said to her husband that he would be with her in the operating room *in spirit,* which means that (he would actually be there/he would think of her while she was there/his ghost would be there).

h. When Beth took a deep breath, she *froze,* which means that (she became very cold/she couldn't move/she couldn't hear or feel anything).

i. The surgeon told Mrs. Mendel that she *gave them a little scare* in the operating room, which means that (they thought she might have died/they thought she might have had a serious operation/they thought her husband had been there in spirit).

2. Match the words which have more or less the *same* meaning.

a. enter	**1.** reply
b. begin	**2.** start
c. answer	**3.** go in
d. want	**4.** feel
e. operate	**5.** desire
f. scare	**6.** make afraid
g. let	**7.** perform surgery
	8. allow

3. Match the *opposites.*

a. crazy	**1.** late
b. wrong	**2.** sensible
c. strong	**3.** right
d. early	**4.** weak
e. nervous	**5.** first
f. last	**6.** soft
	7. calm

C. Discussion or writing practice.

1. What *actions* of her husband's do you think led Beth to believe that he had one of his *feelings?*
2. Do you think it is common for two people who know each other well to know from actions what each other is thinking? Explain.

3. Why didn't he tell his wife what his strange feeling was?
4. Do you think Tom should have told his wife what his strange *feeling* was? Why or why not?
5. What kind of a *picture* do you get of Tom Mendel in this story?
6. Do you think Tom and Beth Mendel had a good relationship? Explain.
7. Why do you think Tom felt so nervous when he sat down in the coffee shop?
8. Imagine that Tom Mendel and the orderly went back to the coffee shop later, where Tom explained what happened. Make up a dialogue between the two.
9. From what you know in the story, how do you explain Tom Mendel's "presence" in the operating room?
10. Tell the class of a similar strange occurrence which you know about or have experienced yourself.

D.   A bit of humor.

1.   An old man, who was in the operating room of a hospital for the first time, was visibly afraid. He looked around nervously at the doctors, nurses, and attendants, who were all wearing white coats, masks, head covers, and gloves, and said, "With all of you dressed alike, how do we know who is to blame if something goes wrong?"

2.   An old man was boasting about the town's physician to a new resident. "Doc is really good at telling what sickness you have," he said. "And, if you die, by golly, that's what you die of."

3.   Some people say today that if you're not too sick when you're in the hospital, you will be when you get the bill.

4.   After examining a hospital patient one morning to check his progress, the doctor went out of the room and said to his wife, "I don't like how your husband looks, Mrs. White."

"Neither do I," came the reply. "But he's so nice to the kids."

Patrick Hannigan

Based on a story from Ireland.

Patrick Hannigan lived all his life with his mother in Galway, on the west coast of Ireland. His father fell in battle in 1917, in World War I, when Patrick was only six years old. The boy's mother, though only thirty at the time, chose not to remarry after her husband's death.
5 Instead, she devoted her life to rearing Patrick, her only son.

Although she had to work very hard to support herself and her son, Widow Hannigan did well in bringing up Patrick. When he became a young man, everyone who knew him liked and respected him. Children looked up to him, women liked his pleasant disposition and smile, and
10 men enjoyed his friendship. Mrs. Hannigan was justly proud of her son.

One October day in 1935 young Patrick Hannigan found himself walking along the street in the bustling traffic on Eyer Square. The place was very familiar to him, but he could not remember how he got there or why. "I must be walking in my sleep," he said to himself. Then
15 he looked into the sky and said, "But how can that be? It appears to be the middle of the day."

Just then two women from the office where Patrick worked walked toward him, chatting together about what they were going to wear to a funeral that afternoon. Wanting to make conversation, Patrick stopped
20 as they approached and took off his cap. "Excuse me," he said, "would you tell me the time?" To his great surprise, when the women stopped in front of him and looked into his face, they both screamed and ran away. One of them stumbled and almost fell down as she ran.

"How strange!" Patrick muttered under his breath. "They must have thought I was some man who was trying to be forward with them. 25 However, he saw some more mysterious reactions to his presence in the next few minutes. A secretary at the factory where his mother worked ducked into a doorway like a frightened cat when she saw him. A man who lived next door to Patrick and his mother almost fell into a store window when Patrick simply said to him, "Hello, Mr. O'Shea. How are 30 you today?" And when a young priest from the local parish saw Patrick wave to him and heard him call, "Greetings, Father!" he crossed himself and muttered something as he hurried across the street, through the traffic, in the middle of the block.

Patrick Hannigan didn't know what to make of all this. "I can't figure it 35 out," he said aloud to himself, as he stood for a moment on the corner. "Yesterday these people were my friends, but today they act as if I have a contagious disease. I wonder what has changed them?" He shook his head as he looked up and down the street for others he might know, saying over and over to himself, "What's the matter? What *is* the matter?" 40

Just then a taxi stopped near where Patrick was walking. When he recognized the driver, Patrick called to him, "Tom! Tom, old boy, are you going my way?" Anxious to have a fare, the taxi driver jumped out of the car and opened the rear door for Patrick. "Tom," said Patrick, as he approached, "please take me home. I'm having a little trouble today. 45 Some of my friends . . ." Patrick didn't get a chance to finish the sentence. When Tom saw who was about to get into his cab, he jumped into the driver's seat and sped away, leaving the back door swinging.

By this time Patrick's head was spinning. He simply could not believe what he had just seen. Tom, who was a friend of the family, was acting 50 like the others. "What on earth is happening? Am I losing my mind or is this a bad dream?" He thought for a minute and then exclaimed, "That's it! It's a dream! I'll wake up in a minute, laugh about all this, and wonder how I could dream about such silly things!" However, minutes passed by and there was no waking up. The people in the street, the smell of 55 the traffic, and the cool breeze on his face convinced him that this was not a dream. But, then, what was it?

He stepped into a nearby chemist's shop,* walked over to the public telephone on the wall, and called his mother. The voice at the other end of the line sounded like that of his mother's sister. "Yes, Mrs. Hannigan 60

---

*In the United States, this would be a *drug store* or *pharmacy.*

is here," came the reply, "but she can't speak to you right now. You see, her only son, Patrick, died in a terrible accident yesterday over on Eyer Square. Mrs. Hannigan, the poor dear," she went on, "is getting ready for the funeral. It's at four o'clock today. If you . . ." Then she heard a
65   *clunk* at the other end of the line. "Hello, sir," she said, "are you still there?" As she took the receiver away from her ear, she said to Mrs. Hannigan, "That's strange! It seemed like that man dropped the receiver when I told him about Patrick's death. The news must have shocked him terribly."
70   "Who was it?" asked Mrs. Hannigan. "Did he say?"

"No, he didn't," she answered with a puzzled look on her face, but somehow that voice *did* sound familiar. I wonder whose it was."

The man working in the shop from where Patrick made the call heard the *clunk* of the falling receiver, too. "Well, now," he said, as he ap-
75   proached the telephone, "I wonder how that receiver got off the hook. I didn't see anyone here, making a call."

A.   Questions on the content of the story.

   1. Where did Patrick and his mother live at the time of this story?
   2. How long had Patrick lived there?
   3. In what year did Patrick's father die?
   4. How long had Patrick lived when his father died?
   5. How old was Patrick's mother when she gave birth to Patrick?
   6. How many other children did Mrs. Hannigan have?
   7. How soon after her husband's death did Patrick's mother marry again?
   8. How long ago did Patrick die? (Figure this date from the time that you are reading this question.)
   9. How old was Patrick at the time of his death? How old was his mother?
  10. When Patrick met the two women from the office where he worked, what did he ask them?
  11. When did the women scream and run away?
  12. Who else did strange things when he or she saw Patrick that day?
  13. What did Patrick ask the taxi driver to do?
  14. What did Patrick do in the chemist's shop?
  15. Why didn't Patrick's mother speak to him when he called?

B.   Vocabulary practice.

   1. Underline the best answer.
      a. Patrick's father *fell in battle*, which means that (he died while fighting in war/he fell over dead/he died in the war because of a fall).
      b. Mrs. Hannigan *devoted her life to rearing Patrick*, which means that (she loved her son very much/she reared her son as a devout person/she spent her life bringing up her son).
      c. Children *looked up to Patrick*, which means that (he was much bigger than the children/ children respected him/children liked to look at him).
      d. One day Patrick *found himself* walking along the street, which means that (he realized where he was/he had been lost/he had died).
      e. The two women were *chatting together* as they walked, which means they were (arguing/talking/singing) together.
      f. One woman ducked into a doorway *like a frightened cat* when she saw Patrick, which means that she got out of his way (like an angry cat/like a scared cat/like a frisky cat).
      g. The young priest who saw Patrick *crossed himself*, which means that (he made the sign of the cross on his own body/he took a cross out of his pocket and held it against himself/he himself crossed the street).
      h. Patrick *didn't know what to make of all this*, which means (he couldn't understand what was happening/he couldn't decide what was happening/he couldn't make things happen).
      i. Patrick's *head was spinning* after Tom, the taxi driver, sped away from him, which means that (his head was shaking/his head was turning round and round/he had a feeling of confusion).
      j. Patrick's voice *sounded familiar* to the woman who answered the phone for Mrs. Hannigan, which means that (it sounded like someone in the family/it sounded like a voice she knew/it sounded strange).
   2. Practice with *rear* and *raise*.
      In some English-speaking countries, it is considered more correct to use *rear* when speaking of bringing up children and

raise when speaking of breeding and bringing animals to maturity or growing plants or trees.

Examples: We want to _rear_ our children correctly.
It's not difficult to _raise_ chickens.
We have to _raise_ more corn next year.

Choose the correct answer.

   a. Do the farmer's in your country (rear/raise) wheat?
   b. My parents (raised/ reared) all ten of us children in a very small house.
   c. They (rear/raise) a lot of cotton in Arizona and Texas.
   d. Patrick's mother (raised/reared) him the best she could.
   e. While she was (raising/rearing) Patrick, she was also working in a factory.
   f. Many people have been (raised/reared) in small towns.
   g. Some parents do not know how to (raise/rear) their sons and daughters.
   h. How many of your brothers and sisters have been (raised/reared) by your grandparents?
3. In English we often use a preposition with a verb to give it a special meaning. There are some of these words in this story.

Examples: Children _looked up_ to Patrick.
The girls _ran away_ when they saw him.
Patrick couldn't _figure out_ what was happening.
Tom was about to _get in_ when the taxi driver saw who he was.

Choose from one of these prepositions to give the sentence the correct meaning: *off, in, out, away, down, up*

   a. Did Patrick take _____ his cap?

   b. He opened the door of the car and said, "Get _____ and let's go!"

   c. He opened the door and said to the boy, "Get _____ and stay out!"

   d. Did the boy run _____ from home?

   e. She fell _____ in the street as she tried to run away.

f. Patrick thought he would wake _____ and find that this was a bad dream.

g. Did you find _____ what happened?

h. I wish he would get _____ my back and leave me alone.

i. She brought _____ her son in the best way she could.

j. Finally, I figured _____ what happened.

k. Did your car break _____ again?

l. My brother and I grew _____ in Minnesota.

m. Didn't they catch _____ with their friends?

n. All children should look _____ to their parents.

4. Match the *opposites.*

a. west	**1.** strange
b. north	**2.** south
c. familiar	**3.** low
d. high	**4.** east
e. near	**5.** silly
f. bad	**6.** good
	7. far

C. Grammar practice.

Choose the correct form of the verb. (Look for indications in the sentence of what the word should be.)

1. Patrick was six years old when his father (dies/died).
2. Patrick's mother did not (remarried/remarry).
3. His mother (reared/rearing) her son alone after her husband died.
4. Patrick died when he (is/was) a young man.
5. The priest was (crossed/crossing) himself while he was running through the traffic.
6. Patrick couldn't (understood/understand) what was happening.
7. Everyone (does/did) strange things when they saw him.
8. Patrick (speak/spoke) to himself as he stood on the corner.

9. He decided to (call/called) his mother.
10. He went into a shop to (make/made) the call.
11. Mrs. Hannigan's sister (answered/answer) the telephone when it rang.
12. Mrs. Hannigan was (getting/got) ready for the funeral when the phone rang.
13. When the woman spoke of Patrick's death, the telephone receiver (dropped/drop).
14. The voice on the phone did (seem/seemed) familiar.
15. The man in the shop didn't (knew/know) how the phone got off the hook.

D. Questions for discussion.

1. On which side do you think Patrick's father was fighting when he fell in battle in World War I?
2. Do you think Mrs. Hannigan was a wealthy woman? Explain.
3. Why did Patrick think he perhaps was walking in his sleep?
4. Why do you think Patrick took off his cap when he asked the women what time it was?
5. Whose funeral do you think the women were planning to attend?
6. Why did they scream when they recognized Patrick?
7. What did Patrick mean when he said the people acted like he had a contagious disease?
8. Do you think many people knew of Patrick's death? Explain.
9. Do you think any of these people told Mrs. Hannigan later that they saw Patrick after his death? Explain.
10. What do you think the priest muttered to himself when he hurried across the street?

E. Storytelling and more conversation practice.

1. Tell the story in your own words. (One person can start, then point to another person to continue, and so on.)
2. In some cultures, there is the belief that the spirit of a person who dies violently remains in the place where he or she died. Explain what you know about this belief or something similar to it.
3. If you know of a story like this or of an occurrence similar to this, tell it to the class.

F.   Writing practice (or more conversation).

1. Write a paragraph about (or tell the class) what kind of a person you think Mrs. Hannigan was.
2. Let's suppose that Tom, the taxi driver, went to see a priest that afternoon about what he saw and that the priest happened to be the one who also saw Patrick.
   a. Write what you think Tom told the priest.
   b. Do you think the priest would have told Tom that he also saw Patrick? Why or why not?
   c. Write a conversation of what you think these two said to each other.
3. Let's suppose you were a newspaper reporter in this city at this time and that you interviewed some of the people who saw Patrick. Write a short article about it.

G.   A bit of humor.

1. A boy about ten years old was telling another boy that he had just seen a ghost.

   First Boy: I'm telling you, I just saw a ghost, and he came after me!
   Second Boy: What did you do?
   First Boy: I ran! I ran as fast as I could! I looked back once and saw him again!
   Second Boy: What was he doing when you looked back?
   First Boy: He was falling behind! Man, he was falling behind *fast!*

Fear

Based on an incident related by a student from Puebla, Mexico.

Armando Gonzalez entered a large bank in Mexico City. After waiting a few minutes in line, he handed the bank teller his savings account passbook and a withdrawal slip.

"Let me see," said the teller, "you want to withdraw 50,000 pesos."

"That's right," answered Armando timidly, as he looked around to see 5 who was watching or listening.

"And do you want a cashier's check for that amount?"

"I'll take it in cash, please," replied Armando.

"A cashier's check is as good as cash, you know, Mr. Gonzalez, and safer." 10

"I know, I know," said Armando, "but I need to have the cash."

"Is it all right, then, if I give it to you in 1,000-peso bills?"

"Yes, yes, that's all right."

Armando was getting more nervous by the minute. He wondered why the woman had to ask so many questions. And why did she speak 15 louder each time she spoke? It seemed to him that half of the people in the bank lobby were looking at him.

The women counted out the bills: "1,000, 2,000, 3,000, 4,000 . . ." Why did she have to say *thousand* each time? "Those people standing behind me in line know exactly how much I'm going to carry in cash," 20 he thought to himself. He fidgeted with his hat in his hands as she finished counting.

". . . 48,000, 49,000, 50,000. There you are, Mr. Gonzalez. Your account now shows a balance of 132 pesos."

25   "Yes, I understand," he said impatiently. His hands shook as he
folded the bills and put them into a front pocket in his baggy pants.

As he turned to leave, he accidentally put his hat on backwards. A
number of the people noticed, and a few of them did a double take. One
rather heavy man almost ran into a table in the middle of the large bank
30   lobby when he looked at Armando a second time. When Armando saw
the man look at him, he felt his hands tremble.

It seemed to him that everyone he saw knew what he had in his
pocket. His palms were so sweaty that they slipped on the big door of
the bank when he pushed it to leave. Also, his mouth felt as dry as dust,
35   his stomach felt like a volcano about to erupt, and his heart was beating
so hard he could feel it in his head.

He stood in the street trying to remember where he was supposed to
go, all the time clutching the wad of bills in his pants pocket.

Fifty thousand pesos* wasn't *all the money in Mexico*, he realized,
40   but it was *all the money in the world* to him and his dear wife, Eva. It
had taken them almost twenty years to save that amount, little by little.
How difficult it was to save anything on what he earned working in a
shoe shop, especially with six children and a mother-in-law at home to
feed and clothe! And it was even more difficult to save anything from the
45   few pesos Eva earned each day taking care of children while their moth-
ers worked cleaning houses.

The 50,000 pesos which Armando held tightly in his pocket was going
to buy a house for the family. Not a beautiful house, as the world judges
beauty, but beautiful to the Gonzalez family because it would be their
50   own. Also, it would be wonderful to have a larger house than the little
one with only three rooms in which they had all lived for so many years.

When Armando and Eva decided to buy the house, they said it was
the happiest day of their lives because they had always dreamed of
having a house of their own. However, Armando did not feel happy
55   right at this moment because the whole dream was in a wad of fifty 1,000
peso bills in the pocket of the worn-out pants he was wearing. And he
realized that someone could take that dream away from him very easily.

"Maybe it would have been better to take the check," he said to
himself as he felt sweat roll down his brow. "As the woman said, it's
60   safer. But then the man who was going to handle the papers for purchasing the house said to bring *the money*, and money means *cash*, doesn't
it?"

*In 1973, when this incident took place, the value of the peso was eight cents in U.S. currency.
One thousand pesos, therefore, was equal to eighty dollars, and 50,000 pesos was equal to 4,000
dollars.

As he gathered his thoughts enough to look for the right bus, he noticed a heavy man standing next to him. He started to shake all over because he was sure it was the man who had looked at him twice in the 65 bank. His legs felt weak, and he could feel his heart beat faster again.

"He's following me, I'm sure," he thought, "but he's acting like he doesn't notice me. How clever!" Armando saw the heavy man put his hand in the inside pocket of his coat. He tried not to notice. "He's probably checking to see if his pistol is still there, the one he's going to 70 use to hold me up when he gets a chance!"

The bus came and Armando got on. Sure enough, the heavy man boarded the bus too. Armando took the first seat he found—right behind the driver. The heavy man took a seat farther back. When others came into the bus, some of them took a look at Armando because he still 75 had his hat on backwards.

"Why do people keep looking at me?" he thought. "Do they all know I have this money in my pocket?" Then he looked into the big mirror over the bus driver's head and saw the heavy man reading a newspaper. "*He* knows for sure!" thought Armando. "I wonder what he has up his 80 sleeve."

As the bus rolled through the city, Armando was so nervous he couldn't think straight. He knew somehow that he had to do some planning of his own to outsmart the man. Finally he came up with an idea. He would leave the bus quickly at one of the next stops and wait 85 for another bus. But what if the man follows? Maybe this situation would be worse. Armando took one more quick look at the heavy man. "He's a crook all right!" he thought. "He's even wearing a black hat. He probably makes a good living robbing people after they come from the bank!" Nervously, Armando reached for the cord for the buzzer, but then held 90 back because he saw three teenage boys talk with the heavy man. "They're probably his helpers!" thought Armando. "I've got to get out of here!"

He grabbed the cord and pulled it quickly. Then, when the bus slowed to a stop, he jumped up and got off through the front door. He 95 felt good for a moment because it looked like he was the only person getting off. Then, to his great surprise, he saw the three boys come out of the bus through the rear door. Feelings of hot and cold ran through his body as the bus pulled away, especially when he noticed that he was in an area with no buildings nearby. 100

The three boys stood and spoke together. Armando couldn't hear what they were saying. Then they all looked in the direction of Armando and started walking toward him. "They're after me!" he thought. "They'll

beat me and take my money! What can I do? Where can I go? The worst
105 has happened!"

He let out a frantic cry and started to run wildly. "Help me somebody!" he shouted at the top of his voice. "Help me, please!"

One of the boys said something to the others. Then they started after
Armando. Armando ran across the street, through a barbed-wire fence,
110 into an old junk yard. He scratched his arm and tore his pants, but got
up and ran faster. He stumbled over a pile of old parts of wrecked cars,
banging against pieces of steel, tin, and glass. Nearby, several scav-
engers were going through the things in the piles. "Help me!" Armando
called, but the noise they made by moving the pieces of metal kept
115 them from hearing him. Then he tripped over some tangled wire and
fell to the ground.

As Armando started to get up, the three boys came over a pile of
metal pieces and approached him cautiously.

He cried like a baby. "Why don't you leave me alone?" he wept. "I'm
120 an honest man. More honest than you could know! I earned all of this
money through hard work!"

"Is there something we can do to help you?" asked one of the boys.

"What?" whimpered Armando in surprise.

"Is there something we can do to help you?" the boy repeated.

125 "You're not here to rob me?"

"No sir," said another of the boys. "We heard you yell for help over
there and decided to try to see if there was anything we could do."

"It sounded like you were out of your head," said another of the boys.

"Who are you?" Armando asked.

130 "We're from Puebla, sir," answered one of the boys. "We're in the
capital for a football tournament."

"You're not part of a street gang?"

"No, of course not," said another, as all three of them laughed.
"We're students."

135 "You didn't leave the bus when I did just to rob me?"

"No, sir," answered one of the boys. "We got off because we realized
we were on the wrong bus. We wanted to take the next one back into
the city."

"What about the fat man on the bus?"

140 "What do you mean?"

"You're not working for that man you talked to on the bus?"

"No, sir. We just asked him about the buses. He told us which one to
take back."

"Oh, really?" said Armando.

Then all four of them walked together back to the street. And, for the first time in the last hour, Armando did not have a sweaty hand in his pocket. Instead, he used both hands to put on his hat, and this time he got it on straight. 145

A.   Questions on the content of the story.

1. In which city did this incident take place?
2. How much money did Armando Gonzalez withdraw from his savings account?
3. How many *bills* did the bank teller give Armando?
4. What was the value, in U.S. currency, of what he had left in the bank after he withdrew 50,000 pesos? (See the footnote on page 106, for help.)
5. Where did Armando work?
6. How did his wife Eva earn a little money?
7. What were Armando and Eva Gonzalez going to buy with this money?
8. As Armando waited for the bus in the street, why wasn't he happy about buying a new house?
9. For what reason did he think the heavy man got on the bus?
10. What did he think the heavy man had in his pocket?
11. Why did some people in the bus look at Armando?
12. What did *Armando* think was the reason they looked at him?
13. Who talked with the heavy man on the bus?
14. Who did Armando think the boys were?
15. Why did Armando leave the bus?
16. Who got off the bus at the same place?
17. Why did Armando cry for help?
18. Where did he run?
19. Why did the boys follow him?
20. Who were the boys?

B.   Vocabulary practice.

1. Underline the best answer.
   a. A bank *teller* is a person in the bank who (tells customers how much money they have/handles money directly with customers, paying and receiving/counts money).
   b. Armando *fidgeted with his hat,* which means that he (played nervously with his hat/put his hat on backwards/ clutched his hat in his sweaty hands).

    c. Some people did a *double take* when they saw that Armando had his hat on backwards, which means that (they thought they saw double/they doubled up with laughter when they saw him/they looked back quickly a second time after they glanced at him).

    d. Armando *clutched* the wad of bills in his pocket, which means that (he folded them together/he held them tightly/he had them in his pocket).

    e. Armando thought the heavy man was going to *hold him up*, which means that he thought the man was going to (rob him/keep him from falling/shoot him).

    f. Armando wondered what the heavy man *had up his sleeve*, which means that he wondered (what he had hidden in his sleeve/if he had a gun/what trick he planned to play on him).

    g. A *crook* is a (dishonest person/person who wears a black hat/heavy person who robs people).

    h. The bus *pulled away* from where Armando was standing, which means that (it towed something behind it/it went fast/it left).

    j. The boys thought Armando was *out of his head*, which means that they thought (he lost his mind/he had his hat on backwards/he was very nervous).

2. Match the words or expressions with more or less the *same meaning*.

a. buy	1. tremble
b. shake	2. leave
c. board	3. get on
d. shout	4. get off
e. pull away	5. take out
f. withdraw	6. purchase
g. reply	7. yell
	8. answer

3. Match the *opposites*.

a. get on	1. ask
b. withdraw	2. get off
c. answer	3. board
d. buy	4. sell
e. start	5. stop
f. push	6. deposit
	7. pull

C.   Grammar practice.

   1. Practice with adjectives.

In English there are two ways to form the comparison of adjectives. One way is by adding *er* and *est*. The other is by using *more* and *most* (usually with longer words). Then there are some words which are *irregular*.

Examples with *er* and *est*.

adjective	comparative form	superlative form
loud	louder	loudest
heavy	heavier*	heaviest
fast	faster	fastest
hard	harder	hardest

Examples with *more* and *most*.

honest	more honest	most honest
beautiful	more beautiful	most beautiful
nervous	more nervous	most nervous
difficult	more difficult	most difficult

Irregular adjectives.

good	better	best
far	farther	farthest

Write the correct form of the adjective in the blank. (Be sure to use *more* and *most* with those words that need it.)

   a. The girl spoke in a _____ voice.
                             (loud)

   b. He was the _____ person in the bank.
                        (nervous)

   c. The man with the black hat was _____
                                    (heavy)
     than Armando.

   d. A cashier's check is _____ than cash.
                       (good)

*Take care to change *y* to *i* if necessary.

e. He did not think this girl was the _____

(good)

teller in the bank.

f. The money was _____ in the bank than

(safe)

in Armando's pocket.

g. It is very _____ to act calm when you

(difficult)

feel nervous.

h. A house which you own, seems _____

(beautiful)

than one you only rent.

i. Did you say that it was the _____ day

(happy)

of their lives?

j. When he saw the heavy man, his legs felt _____

(weak)

_____ than they ever had before.

k. Is that boy the _____ runner on the

(fast)

team?

l. After one _____ look at the man, Ar-

(quick)

mando jumped off the bus.

m. This bus is _____ than the other one.

(fast)

n. Armando is the _____ man I know.

(honest)

o. He felt _____ when he left the junk

(good)

yard than when he had entered.

2. Practice with verbs. Write the correct verb in the blank. (Look
   for indications of *tense* in the sentence.)

   a. Armando _____ the money yesterday.

   (withdraw)

b. Were you _____ at him while he was
    (look)

standing in line?

c. How much money did he _____ out of
    (take)

his account?

d. Armando looked around while she _____
    (count)

the money.

e. Mr. and Mrs. Gonzalez have not _____
    (buy)

the house yet.

f. He had always _____ that the worst
    (think)

would happen.

g. When he left the bus, he did not know that the boys had

_____ off, too.
    (get)

h. As he stood in the street, his hands _____.
    (shake)

i. When Armando works, he always _____
    (try)

to do his best.

j. While the children grew up, the Gonzalez family

_____ in a small house.
    (live)

k. He had _____ weak ever since he left
    (feel)

the bank.

l. When he saw the man, his legs _____
    (feel)

weak.

m. I hope he doesn't _____ how much
    (notice)

money he has.

n. When Armando _____ nervous, he
(feel)

shows it.

o. I reached for the cord and _____ it.
(grab)

p. The boys did not _____ him.
(rob)

D. Questions for discussion.

(Divide into small groups, if possible).

1. Why did Armando have the idea that everyone in the bank was watching him? What was the truth?
2. Armando said that the man who was going to help him with the purchase of the house told him to bring *the money,* and he thought that this meant he had to bring *cash.* Do you think he was right about that? Explain.
3. If someone had told him that his hat was on backwards when he left the bank, do you think that Armando would have felt better? Explain.
4. What are some things which made Armando think that some-one was going to rob him?
5. Do you think we sometimes make things *worse* rather than *better* when we get nervous? Explain.
6. How do you think Armando felt when he found out that the boys wanted to help him? What do you think he said to them?

E. More discussion or writing practice.

1. Write a paragraph (or tell the class) about a time you, or some-one you know, became nervous unnecessarily.
2. Many people have different *physical things* happen to them when they get nervous. Write a paragraph about (or tell the class) some things that happen to you when you get nervous.
3. Write a paragraph (or tell the class) about *what a person can do to bring nervous tension under control.*
4. Write a paragraph (or tell the class) about what *you* think *you* would have done if you and two friends had been the three who were there when Armando started to run and cry for help.
5. Let's suppose that Armando finally arrived home safely after

taking care of everything concerning the purchase of the house. Write a paragraph (or tell the class) about what you think he told his wife, if anything, about his experience. If you do *not* think he told her, explain why you think he didn't.

6. This story tells only about something that happened in approximately *one hour* of Armando's life. Write a paragraph about (or tell the class) what kind of a person you think Armando really was.

F.   A bit of humor.

Anyone who has been in a foreign country, not knowing the language, will appreciate this story, which has been told many times in Mexico.

A very shy man from Mexico once had to make a business trip to the United States, but he knew *no* English. Upon his return, he told one of his friends that the bad part of his trip was that he ate nothing but *coffee* and *doughnuts* for the entire five days.

"Why?" asked the friend.

"That's all I knew."

"Didn't you try?"

"Well, yes I did," he replied. "After three days, I sat at the counter in a restaurant and heard the man next to me say, 'I'll have a steak.' They brought him steak, potatoes, vegetables, and everything. So, I said the same thing to the waitress, 'I'll have a steak.'"

She answered, going 100 kilometers per hour, "Would you like rib steak? T-bone? Porterhouse? You want it rare? Medium? A baked potato? French fries? What will you have?"

"'Coffee and doughnuts' was all I could answer, so that's what I got."

The Little
Christmas Visitor

Based on an incident told by a student from France.

"Are you sure we did the right thing in moving into this old house," I asked my wife, Celeste, after the last of the furniture was carried in.

"Yes, Pierre, my love, I am," she said happily as she took my hand. "There is not a doubt in my mind. Furthermore, it's paid for. Isn't that nice? After all, you weren't paid much for your writing in the past 5 months, and I haven't sold a painting since summer."

"I guess you're right," I said, as I smiled. "At least we have a place to live not far from Paris. And I'll have to admit that this house seems to have more character than the uncle who left it to me."

"I love it!" Celeste replied as I held her in my arms. "I think it's going 10 to be a good place to live and a great place to work!"

"So, the stories we were told about the house don't bother you?"

"They don't scare me a bit," she laughed. Then she looked into my eyes and said seriously, "Really, Pierre, we may be somewhat poor because of our circumstances, but we're not ignorant. We know that 15 there is a reason for everything!"

"Everything?" I asked, raising my eyebrows.

"Yes, everything!" she said. "And it's 1955; we're not living in the Middle Ages! But if it will make you feel better, we'll have the house blessed by a priest as soon as we get settled." 20

"Which reminds me," I said as I looked around at the piles of boxes. "We have to get busy if we are going to have things in place by Christmas. That's only ten days away!"

We did get busy, and things were quite well organized in the big, old

25 house by the day before Christmas. We even had time to put up a small
Christmas tree in the parlor which, to the great delight of our three-year
old daughter, Michelle, was decorated with dozens of tiny dolls and
elves in colorful dress, all handmade by Celeste.

On Christmas Eve, after the last gift was wrapped and put under the
30 tree, Celeste sat down in a comfortable chair to admire the tree. I had
put Michelle to bed and was getting ready for bed myself.

As Celeste gazed at the tree, thinking of Christmases she enjoyed so
much on the farm in the mountains of France, where she grew up, she
dozed off. Suddenly she was awakened by the whimpering of a child.
35 Thinking it was our daughter, she started to get up out of the chair to go
to her bedroom. Then her heart almost stopped as a chill ran through
·   her body! There, just a few feet in front of her, was a child, which was
definitely not Michelle! It looked like a little boy, about five years old, in
night clothes of a very old style. He cried softly as he touched the
40 packages under the tree, one by one, not seeming to notice that there
was someone in the room with him.

Celeste gathered her thoughts enough to want to find out who this
was. She leaned forward in the chair and said, "Are you looking for
something, little boy?"
45 With that, the child turned and faced her. Seemingly more frightened than she, he started to back up into the tree, but not one branch or
ornament moved! Then he disappeared right into the tree!

Celeste came running into the bedroom where I lay on the bed
waiting for her, almost asleep.
50 "Pierre!" she exclaimed in a loud whisper. "I think I just saw a ghost!"

"A ghost?" I asked, opening my eyes in disbelief. "Tell me that you're
joking, and then come to bed. I'm really tired." I rolled over in the bed
and closed my eyes again.

"Pierre, please listen to me!" she insisted. "I think I just saw a ghost."
55 Realizing that she was serious, I sat up and listened to her story.

The day after Christmas the house was blessed by the priest, and we
thought little more about our Christmas visitor. In fact, the old house
seemed like a good place for us. I wrote a number of stories in the next
months which were purchased by magazines. I even won a prize with
60 one of them. Also, Celeste sold a number of her paintings and finished
more.

The next Christmas, Celeste's mother came to spend the holidays
with us. She was seeing the house for the first time and was delighted by
it. For various reasons, we did not tell her about the little visitor we had
65 had the Christmas before.

Christmas Eve, after we had put Michelle to bed, Celeste, her mother, and I decided to finish a few last things for the Christmas dinner for the next day. Celeste's mother took a few apples to peel and sat down with them in her lap in the parlor near the Christmas tree, enjoying the warmth of the fire.   70

All of a sudden we heard a sound from her which made both Celeste and me think she was choking. We both ran into the parlor where we saw her sitting, looking as white as a sheet. The apples were rolling on the floor.

"I—I just s-saw s-something," she stammered. Then she calmed   75
down enough to tell us what she saw. It quite evidently was the same thing Celeste had seen on Christmas Eve a year before.

Needless to say, the three of us sat and talked for hours, trying to reason this thing out. Celeste's mother, who almost *never* drinks, even had a glass of brandy with us.   80

The next Sunday we had the priest over for dinner. Again he blessed the house, after we told him what had happened. The priest had no answers for us but suggested that we find out more about the house.

About a month later I found a woman in Paris who knew something about the old house. She was over ninety, but her mind was as clear as a   85
bell. She told me that before my uncle had purchased the house, it was owned by a rich man whose five-year-old son had died there—of neglect, she said, in spite of the wealth of the parents. The old woman also told me that this couple objected to the celebration of Christmas because a business of theirs had at one time burned down on Christmas   90
night.

It was all very interesting, but I thought little more about it because I was so busy with my work.

The next Christmas Eve, when our little girl was five, she and I were sitting in front of the fireplace, near the Christmas tree, reading the   95
Christmas story.

Suddenly, out of the corner of my eye, I saw someone by the Christmas tree. I looked and saw what seemed to be the same child seen by my wife and mother-in-law before. I tried to observe him as carefully as I could. He was doing the same thing as before—crying softly and   100
touching the packages under the tree.

When Michelle saw the little boy, she got up off my lap and approached him. Since she had never heard us talk about our experiences with this boy on previous occasions, she thought he was *just another child*. To my great surprise, the child did not retreat from her as he had   105
from us.

"Why are you crying, little boy?" Michelle asked him. "Don't you know that Christmas is a happy time?"

The little boy stood still and looked at her, his tear-filled eyes
110 glistening.

"Christmas is Jesus' birthday. Don't you know that?" Then she proceeded to tell him the story of Christmas that I had just read to her. After a few minutes she concluded, "And so you see, we give gifts to each other at Christmas because God gave His Son, Jesus, to the world." With that she
115 took him by the hand and stood with him in front of the tree, looking at the gaily wrapped packages and the colorful decorations. "Isn't Christmas beautiful?" she said.

When Michelle ran to another room to tell her mother about the little boy, the child took a look at me, smiled faintly, and disappeared into the
120 tree.

Michelle came running back into the room in a minute, followed by Celeste. "Where is he?" she asked excitedly as she looked around the room. I was still sitting in the chair, a little stunned by what I had just seen.
125 "I think he has gone home, sweetheart," I said to Michelle, taking her onto my lap again. "That was very nice of you to tell him the story of Christmas. I think now maybe he has gone home to celebrate Jesus' birthday himself."

I held Michelle close as Celeste and I looked at each other, not
130 knowing what to say. Then Michelle looked up at me and asked, "Daddy, why was that boy's hand so cold?"

I'm sure my attempt at an explanation at a child's level was meaningless to her. However, what she said to that little Christmas visitor must have been meaningful to him, for he never came back to whimper
135 under our tree again, nor did we have any more visitors like him in the twenty years we lived in that house.

A.   Questions on the content of the story.

1. At the beginning of the story, where were Pierre and Celeste going to live?
2. Where was the house located?
3. Who gave them the house?
4. What year was it when the story began?
5. Which holiday was coming soon?
6. As Celeste sat dozing near the Christmas tree on Christmas Eve, what awakened her?

7. What description did she give of the child she saw?
8. Where did the child go when Celeste spoke to him?
9. What did she tell her husband she had seen?
10. When did they have the house blessed?
11. When did Celeste's mother come to visit them?
12. What did she think of the house?
13. What was Celeste's mother doing when she saw the little boy?
14. Did seeing the boy frighten her? Explain.
15. Who told them to try to find out something about the house?
16. Who told Pierre some things about the house?
17. Who saw the little boy next?
18. What were they doing when they saw him?
19. Who spoke to him?
20. What did she explain to him?
21. Why did little Michelle leave the room?
22. Who came back to the parlor with her?
23. What had happened to the boy in the meantime?
24. How many more times did they see the boy?

B. Vocabulary practice.

1. Underline the best answer.
   a. Celeste said there was *not a doubt in her mind* about moving into this house, which means that (she was sure that they did the right thing/she was not sure they did the right thing/they needed a place to live).
   b. Pierre said that an uncle had *left the house to him*, which means that (the uncle had left before Pierre moved in/ Pierre had inherited the house from an uncle/the house had more character than Pierre's uncle).
   c. To *whimper* means to (cry hard/cry softly/cry while touching something).
   d. A priest *blessed the house*, which means that the priest (came to live with them for awhile/conducted a ceremony in the house in which he asked for God's blessing for the house and the people in it/tried to get the ghosts out of the house).
   d. Celeste *gazed at* the Christmas tree, which means that (she looked at the tree while thinking of past Christmases/she looked at the tree while she dozed off/she looked at it intently).

    e. To *stammer* means to (speak stumblingly/to speak fast/to speak slowly).

    f. The couple *objected to* the celebration of Christmas, which means that they (were against/rejected/neglected) the celebration of Christmas.

    g. Pierre tried *to observe* the little Christmas visitor as carefully as he could, which means that he tried to (look at him/approach him/talk to him) carefully.

    h. *To retreat* means to (give a treat again/draw back/whimper).

    i. Michelle *proceeded* to tell the boy the story of Christmas, which means that she (told him in a soft voice/began to tell him/told him quickly).

2. Match the words or phrases which mean more or less *the same*.

a. finish	**1.** observe
b. buy	**2.** complete
c. watch	**3.** frighten
d. tell	**4.** organize
e. approach	**5.** go toward
f. scare	**6.** purchase
	7. relate

C.   Grammar practice.

   1. Explanation of the passive voice.

   In English sentences, when the subject *performs* or *does* something expressed by a verb, it is the *active voice*.

   Examples: The men carry the furniture.
              Mary drives the car.
              The child speaks English.

   When the subject *receives* the action, it is the *passive* voice.

   Examples: The furniture is carried by the men.
              The car is driven by Mary.
              English is spoken by the child.

   We form sentences with the passive voice by adding the *past participle* of the verb (*spoken, driven, carried,* and so on) to the correct form of the verb *to be*. If we identify the agent, it is preceded by *by*. (See the preceding examples for the passive voice.)

The passive voice may be used also when the agent is not or cannot be identified.

Examples: The car works best when it *is driven* carefully.
When I speak English, I *am* sometimes *misunderstood.*

The passive, like the active voice, may be used with *any tense* of the verb *to be*.

Examples: Present tense
Active voice: *The priest blesses the house.*
Passive voice: *The house is blessed by the priest.*

Past tense
Active voice: *The priest blessed the house.*
Passive voice: *The house was blessed by the priest.*

Future tense
Active voice: *The priest will bless the house.*
Passive voice: *The house will be blessed by the priest.*

2. Practice with the passive voice.
   a. There are sentences using the passive voice in this story.

   Examples: The last of the furniture *was carried* in.
   You *weren*'t *paid* much for your writing.

   Find at least six more sentences which use the passive voice.
   (Remember that they may be in *any* tense.)

   (1) _____

   (2) _____

   (3) _____

   (4) _____

   (5) _____

   (6) _____

b. Complete the following sentences by changing them from the *active* to the *passive voice.*

Examples: I don't sell many paintings.
Not many paintings *are sold by me.*
Someone told stories about the house.
Stories about the house *were told by someone.*
Stories don't scare me.
I am not *scared by stories.*

(1) We decorated the Christmas tree.

The Christmas tree _____

(2) Celeste makes the ornaments for the tree.

The ornaments for the tree _____

(3) We will put the Christmas tree in the parlor.

The Christmas tree _____

(4) The little boy awakened Celeste.

Celeste _____

(5) He touches each of the packages.

Each of the packages _____

(6) The little visitor frightened my mother-in-law.

My mother-in-law _____

(7) All of us saw the ghost.

The ghost _____

(8) He writes many stories.

Many stories _____

(9) The boy will visit us again next year.

We _____

(10) Michelle brought her into the room.

She _____

c. Write the correct form of the verb in the blank. (Look for indications of *tense. Some* will use the form for the *passive voice,* but not all.)

(1) Did they all _____ good work?
(do)

(2) Was good work _____ by all of
      (do)

them?

(3) The house was _____ to him by
      (leave)

his uncle.

(4) When he died, he _____ many
      (leave)

things to the members of his family.

(5) After they moved in, he _____
      (write)

many good stories.

(6) When he works hard, he _____
      (write)

good stories.

(7) Many good stories were _____
      (write)

by him after they moved into the old house.

(8) Stories like that don't _____ me.
      (scare)

(9) I am not easily _____ by stories
      (scare)

like that.

(10) English is _____ at that school.
      (speak)

(11) When I visited that school, all of the students

_____ English.
      (speak)

(12) Were the boys _____ English
      (speak)

when you heard them?

(13) Please _____ English in this class.
      (speak)

(14) Did they _____ a ghost?
      (see)

(15) Was the ghost _____ by all of them?   (see)

(16) Do only certain people _____ ghosts?   (see)

D.   Questions for discussion.

1. What kind of stories do you think they had heard about this house?
2. Do you think they had been told about the little Christmas visitor? Explain.
3. Do Pierre and Celeste seem like superstitious people? Explain.
4. Why do you think the old house was a good place for Pierre and Celeste to work?
5. This story is told by Pierre in the *first person*. Do you think it would be more effective if it were told by a narrator who is not identified? Explain.
6. Why do you think the priest suggested that they try to find out more about the house?
7. Why do you think Celeste and Pierre had not told Celeste's mother about the little Christmas visitor before she came to visit? Why do you think they had not told their little daughter?
8. Do you think little Michelle had been taught anything about the French equivalent of Santa Claus? Explain.
9. Do you think telling the little Christmas visitor about Jesus had more effect than telling him about Santa Claus would have had? Explain.
10. Why do you think the little boy did not return after his third Christmas visit?

E.   Writing practice (or more discussion).

1. Write a paragraph (or tell the class) about what kind of people you think Celeste and Pierre were. (Using your imagination, go beyond what little the story tells about them.)
2. Write a paragraph (or tell the class) about why you think Celeste's mother was more shocked by the experience of seeing the little Christmas visitor than Celeste and Pierre were.
3. Write a paragraph (or tell the class) about how you think *you* would react to seeing a visitor like this boy.

4. Write a paragraph (or tell the class) about a *visitor* like this boy which you have seen or heard of.
5. Write a paragraph (or tell the class) about how you think *you* would have answered little Michelle's question: "Why was the boy's hand so cold?"

F. A bit of humor.

The way a child reasons is sometimes very interesting to adults.

A door-to-door salesperson walked up to a house. Finding a little girl, about five years old, playing on the steps, the salesperson asked, "Is your mother home?"

"Yes, she is," the child answered politely. So the salesperson straightened his tie and rang the doorbell. There was no answer. Again he rang and waited. Then he tried a third time, while the little girl continued to play busily at his feet.

"I thought you said your mother was home," he finally said to the child.

Without looking up, she answered in a very matter-of-fact voice, "My mother *is* home, but this is not where I live."

One morning, as our family was leaving for a week in the mountains, we were saying goodbye to a student from Japan, who was going to stay at our house while we were gone. The student, who had lived with us a number of times during school vacation, had also previously stayed at our house in our absence.

As we were getting into the car, our six-year-old son, who loved the student dearly, said to him, "Do you like to stay at our house when we're gone?"

The student put his hand affectionately on the little boy's head and said, "Yes, I do. But I like it better when you are all here."

"Is it lonely here when we're not here?" he then asked.

Trying to help the student, I answered for him, "I'm sure it's lonely, Jeffrey, but Kunihiko has a lot of things to do and . . ."

"But daddy," our little boy interrupted, "How do *you* know if it's lonely here when we're gone. You've never been here to see."

A four-year-old boy came home from the birthday party of one of his friends in the neighborhood.

"How was the birthday party?" asked the boy's mother.

"Oh, it was okay until Georgie's mother spanked me."

"Spanked you?" asked the mother with a look of surprise. "What did you do?"

"I cried," was the simple answer.

The Whirlpool

Based on a story told by a student from Bangladesh.

I never thought I would be able to pass this way again. At least, not on a panshi* on this wide river, where whirlpools seem to start anywhere, for no reason. But, of course, this boat wasn't quite as small as the one from which my young bride fell, never to be found. Eight oarsmen worked below, rowing this boat; on that one there were only four.   5

What bothered me was that I was again with a bride, a new love. And I was just as happy with Sarajan as I had been with Didi, my first love. "Then why think of the past?" I thought to myself. "Four years is a long time, and time has already healed much of the wound."

As the boat was moved quietly through the water by the skilled   10 oarsmen, Sarajan and I sat in our tiny cabin above in silence. It must have been evident to her that I was lost in thought about what had happened four years before. She moved closer as though to show her love, but what came from her mouth were not words of love. It seemed to me like crazy talk, as though the lips on her pretty face were moved   15 by the devil himself. This was not the Sarajan I knew.

"Do you love me, Mashud?" she asked, moving closer and squeezing my hand.

"Of course, I love you," I replied as I put my arm around her. "Why do you ask? We were just married, weren't we?"   20

"We're near the place, aren't we? That's why you're so quiet, isn't it?"

---

*A panshi is a small passenger boat.

"Near what place?" I said, acting as though I had no idea what she was talking about.

"You know what I mean," she insisted. "The place where your wife
25 drowned."

"Wife?" I said, holding her closer. "You are my only wife. My only love."

"I'm your only wife?" she said, turning her face toward mine. "Are you telling me that you love me more than you did Didi?"

30   "Of course I love you more!" I replied, trying to reassure her. "You are the most beautiful and most intelligent woman I have ever met. I love you more than I could possibly have ever loved anyone else."

I knew immediately that I shouldn't have said that I loved her more than Didi! It wasn't fair to say that just because Sarajan was there and
35 Didi was gone.

"If you love me so much, why aren't you talking more joyfully, Mashud, my love?"

"How can you say that I am not speaking joyfully. I'm on my honeymoon with my beautiful bride. I would be a fool if I did not speak and act
40 with joy."

"Then you are a fool," she answered. "For there certainly is no joy in your words."

I wanted her to stop this nonsense. It was of no value. It was true that my mind was on what had happened four years ago, but I thought she
45 could be understanding about that. After all, the memory was revived by my being on a panshi on the same river. It was not as though I thought about this all the time. I never spoke of Didi with Sarajan unless she asked. And she almost never asked.

"We're right at the place now, aren't we?" she said drawing away
50 from my arms.

I reached for the curtain of the small cabin window beside us to look. She grabbed my arm and pulled it back. "You don't really have to look, do you?" she said very seriously. "You can *feel* it."

As I sat back, my face felt very warm, and I could feel the beat of my
55 heart. "Whatever makes you say that? How could I remember the place? It was stormy and dark. And it's been a long time!"

"You *know* this is the place, don't you?" she insisted. "Your bride is in a grave of sand here, isn't she?"

I felt my body shake. "So what if this is the place? It doesn't matter!" I
60 said excitedly. "She was taken by God! Taken, I suppose, so that I could love you! Don't you see?"

"You don't have to shout at me, Mashud. I am your wife, you know."

I stood up and stepped out onto the small deck in front of the cabin. I was trembling in every part of my body.

"Don't go out there, Mashud, please don't!" she pleaded. "You could be thrown overboard if we hit rough water!"

I needed the air and I needed to get away from her. From all of her crazy talk. "There's no rough water," I assured her. "The moon is bright and the river is like glass." I stood there and breathed deeply.

The boat was gliding smoothly down the wide river, close enough to the shore on one side that I could see the moonlight cast shadows among the big trees on the bank. Some of the shadows seemed weird, even depressing. Then a slight wind began to make the branches on the large trees groan as though they were in pain.

I looked the other way, across the wide expanse of the river. The light of the moon cast a glistening beam across the water. Like a powerful light, it followed us over the surface of the river, going where we went.

I looked back again toward the shadows in the trees. It was then that I saw her! My Didi came floating in the air toward me. Out of the shadows she came! Closer and closer! Was it really Didi? I closed my eyes as I clutched the railing of the boat. Then I opened them again. She was still there! Still coming nearer, her beautiful sari blowing in the breeze!

How I wished I had not said that I loved Sarajan more than her! "I didn't really mean it," I said to myself; "I was forced to say that!"

She moved closer to me through the night until I could almost reach out and touch her. Then she began to call, "Mashi! Mashi!" That voice! That sweet voice! "Mashi, don't leave me here! Take me with you. It has been so long!"

As I reached out to her, I heard one of the men below shout, "Whirlpool! Whirlpool to the right! Turn left! Turn left! We're on the edge of one made by the devil's tail!"

Then I heard Sarajan call from behind me, "Come back, Mashud! Please come back! Please, Mashud!"

Her call and the oarsmen's warnings meant nothing to me because Didi was coming toward me! My Didi was coming to me through the air! How beautiful she looked! I was so close I could see the glow of the vermilion spot on her forehead! I reached out to her. She was so near! So near! I reached out farther. Then, as though in slow motion, I felt the boat turn and move away from me. I fell. I fell right into her arms! Those lovely arms! Nothing else in the world mattered now. Didi and I were together again!

I woke up on the boat landing in a small riverside village. The first rays of sun appeared to be coming through the trees. Several of the boatmen were kneeling around me. I looked up at them in a daze.

105   "Where is she?" I asked. "Where is she?"

"Your wife?" asked one of the men. "She's over there with those women, weeping. She thought you were dead and she keeps saying it was all her fault. I'll go tell her the good news."

As he left, I said to another one of the boatmen, "I heard your
110   warnings, but there wasn't anything I could do when we hit that whirl-pool."

"Whirlpool, sir?" he said with a confused look on his face. "We hit no whirlpool. The river was smooth, we were being pushed by a gentle current, and the breeze was in our favor."

115   I looked up at him almost too surprised to speak. "No—no wh-whirlpool?" I stammered.

"None at all, sir. Your wife said that she saw you reach over the railing on the deck. She said she called to you, but you just muttered something and fell overboard. She didn't push you, did she?"

120   "No," I answered slowly. "No, she didn't."

"Perhaps the whirlpool was in your head, sir," added another of the men with a smile, "because your wife tells us that you are a good swimmer, yet you did nothing to save yourself in the water."

"And you fell only about eight feet down in the water," said another,
125   "missing the oars, the lower deck, and everything. You were not injured in any way, sir."

I still didn't know what to say as I lay there. Then I saw Sarajan running toward me with her arms out, and I was glad to be alive.

A. Questions on the content of the story.

1. Where were Mashud and his bride, Sarajan, as the story began?
2. What was Mashud thinking about as they rode in the panshi down the river? Why?
3. How many men rowed the boat on which Mashud and Sarajan were riding?
4. How long before had Mashud's first wife died? How did she die?
5. What did Sarajan keep asking him about?
6. Why did he tell Sarajan that he loved her more than he loved his first wife?

7. Why was he sorry later that he had said that?
8. What was different about the weather the night Mashud's wife was lost four years before?
9. Why did Mashud go out onto the deck of the boat?
10. What did Mashud see from the two sides of the boat *before* he saw Didi come to him?
11. From which side did he see Didi come? Describe what Mashud thought he saw.
12. Did he hear Didi speak to him? Explain.
13. Who did Mashud think he heard give a warning about the whirlpool?
14. Who else did he hear call to him?
15. Where did Mashud wake up?
16. Why was Sarajan weeping?
17. Who told Mashud that they had not hit a whirlpool?

B. Vocabulary practice.

1. Underline the best answer.
   a. An *oarsman* is a person who (rows a boat/is the pilot of the boat/works on a panshi).
   b. A *whirlpool* is (a whirlwind/water moving rapidly in a circle/a pool of water).
   c. To *reassure* means to (make sure/ give confidence again/ give love again).
   d. A *honeymoon* is (a sweet time/a trip taken by a newly married couple/a trip on a river).
   e. When Sarajan said to Mashud, "Your bride is in *a grave of sand* here," she meant that (her body was at the bottom of the river/she was buried near the river/she was buried in sand).
   f. When Sarajan said to Mashud, "You could be *thrown overboard* if we hit rough water," she meant that (someone could throw him in the river/he could fall off the boat/he could fall into a whirlpool).
   g. When Mashud said that he *clutched* the railing of the boat, he meant that (he reached over the railing/he leaned over the railing/he held on tightly to the railing).
   h. *Vermilion* is (bright red/bright orange/black).
   i. Mashud looked up at the boatmen *in a daze*, which means that he (was confused/realized it was a new day/had boatmen kneeling around him).

    j. When one of the men said to Mashud, "Perhaps *the whirl-pool was in your head*," he meant that Mashud perhaps (was a good swimmer/was confused/fell into a whirlpool).

2. Match the words or phrases which have more or less the *same meaning*.

a. squeeze	**1.** come to life
b. talk	**2.** pull
c. revive	**3.** hold tightly
d. draw	**4.** sense
e. feel	**5.** throw
f. shake	**6.** speak
g. cast	**7.** stammer
	8. tremble

C. Grammar practice. Write the correct form of the verb.

    a. The oarsmen had _____ that way be-
                            (go)
    fore.

    b. Mashud _____ that way before, too.
                     (go)

    c. As he sat in silence, he _____ about what
                               (think)
    happened four years ago.

    d. Mashud did not _____ about what
                            (think)
    happened until he was on the river.

    e. After Didi fell, they never _____ her
                              (find)
    body.

    f. Mashud's body was _____ a few min-
                           (find)
    utes after he fell.

    g. Sarajan had never _____ like this be-
                          (speak)
    fore.

    h. At first they did not _____ to each
                          (speak)
    other.

i. Didi had _____ into the water four
                    (fall)

    years before.

j. Did Mashud _____ into the water,
                    (fall)

    too?

k. Do people _____ from these boats
                    (fall)

    frequently?

l. A person _____ easily, if he or she is
                    (fall)

    not careful.

2. Practice with prepositions. Write *into* or *onto* in the blanks.

  a. They went _____ the small cabin.

  b. He walked out _____ the deck of the boat.

  c. They put him _____ the bank of the river.

  d. They did not want the boat to get _____ a
     whirlpool.

  e. Did the teacher go _____ the classroom?

  f. The boys got _____ an argument.

3. Practice with *tag questions.*

We use *tag questions* to verify something or to get a response
from a listener.

Examples: We were just married, *weren't we?*
           We're near the place, *aren't we?*
           That's why you're quiet, *isn't it?*

  a. Can you find three tag questions used in this story, in
     addition to the preceding?

     (1) _____

     (2) _____

     (3) _____

  b. Write the tag questions for these sentences. Take care to
    notice *the person* and the *verb tense.*

(1) I was there with you, _____?

(2) This is your book, _____?

(3) They are your friends, _____?

(4) You saw him this morning, _____?

(5) We were with you that night, _____?

(6) He can't swim, _____?

(7) I told you, _____?

(8) This is the right book, _____?

(9) We need our books today, _____?

(10) She will be a good teacher, _____?

D. Questions for discussion.

1. Do you think Mashud *wanted* to take his second bride on a trip so similar to the one he took with his first wife? Explain.
2. Do you think being in the place where his first wife died would have bothered him as much if he had been *alone*? Explain.
3. Why do you think Sarajan talked so much about Mashud's first wife?
4. Do you think the behavior of Mashud and Sarajan on this trip was different from their usual behavior? Explain.
5. Why do you think Mashud thought the trees *groaned* as though they were in pain?
6. Do you think when Mashud thought he heard a warning about a whirlpool that his mind may have gone back to *another time* when he *did*, in fact, hear such a warning? Explain.
7. Why do you think Mashud felt as though his fall into the water was in slow motion?
8. Why did Sarajan say that Mashud's fall was *her fault?*
9. Do you think Mashud told Sarajan about seeing Didi? Explain.

E. Writing practice (or further discussion).

1. Write a paragraph describing (or speak to the class about) Sarajan, Mashud, or Didi.
2. Write a paragraph explaining (or speak to the class about) what you think Mashud actually saw when he said Didi was floating

to him through the air. (Was it real? Was it a ghost? Did he imagine it all?) Explain.

3. Write a paragraph explaining (or speak to the class about) what you think Mashud and Sarajan's relationship was *after* this experience.

Dennis O'Day and the Leprechaun

Based on a story from Ireland.

Dennis O'Day learned to read and write when he was a boy, but he was not what you would call a well-educated lad. When he was growing up, he found it much easier to sit under a tree all day than to sit in school a few hours. And after he was old enough to drink legally, he found it much more pleasant to learn from friends in a pub than from the books in the town library. 5

One day, however, when Dennis was about thirty, he did go to the town library to look up something. It had been so long since he had set foot in the library that he admired the new tables, not knowing that they had been purchased ten years before. 10

When Dennis walked up to the librarian, a prim woman who looked like one who knew everything in all the books around her, he tried not to act ignorant. However, it was a little difficult for Dennis to act like he knew something. In fact, it would have been easier for an elephant to act like a kangaroo. After all, when a man has learned most of what he 15 knows from pub philosophers, he's not going to act like he's a professor at the university.

Dennis did the best he could at the moment. He took off his cap, brushed his hair back with his hand, opened his eyes wide, and told the librarian, Miss Reilly, that he wanted to find out something about lep- 20 rechauns. Miss Reilly, who knew Dennis, took a book which was not too difficult to read. Then she even found the place in the book for him. Dennis thanked her, sat down at one of the tables, and started reading. His lips moved as he pushed his fingers along under the words:

25   The leprechaun of Ireland is a mischievous fellow, part spirit and part fairy—a kind of cross between good and evil. People who have seen leprechauns say that they are two to three feet tall and are usually dressed in green jackets, black britches buckled at the knee, and black stockings. Under the jacket is a white shirt with frills, from Elizabethan times.
30   Leprechauns also wear broad-brimmed, high-pointed hats, usually cocked on the side of the head.

Dennis read on laboriously, mouthing the words in a whisper as he moved his finger along under each word, stumbling over any word with more than two syllables:

35   Each leprechaun is reported to carry a purse containing a few gold coins.

"Here it is!" whispered Dennis loud enough for Miss Reilly to look over his way, put her finger to her lips, and frown, like librarians do. Dennis was too interested in what he was reading to worry about disturbing anyone. "Here it is!" he said again in a hoarse whisper. "Here's
40   the part about the money!" Then he read on as quickly as he could, which wasn't very fast:

People say that when the leprechaun uses the coins he has in his purse, there are always more there the next time he opens it.

"Think of it!" Dennis whispered, too loud again. "If I can catch a
45   leprechaun, he could support me nicely for the rest of my born days!" He was going to close the book, but just then he noticed something else:

Those who have tried to catch a leprechaun have usually come to grief in doing so.

"Well, that's not going to happen so easily to me!" said Dennis se-
50   riously. "If Dennis O'Day catches a leprechaun, it's going to be the leprechaun who's going to come to grief!" Then he put his finger to the page and read more:

They say leprechauns have an intense dislike for schoolteachers, probably because teachers tell people not to believe in leprechauns. And, in-
55   terestingly, it has been said that no one with a teacher's license has ever seen a leprechaun—even if he or she had seen one earlier in life.

"When I catch my leprechaun," muttered Dennis to himself, "I'll have to be careful of schoolmaster McClanahan next door."

Dennis gave the book back to Miss Reilly, put on his cap, and left the library to set out on a very serious hunt for a leprechaun. Although he never was what you would call an ambitious man, Dennis worked very ambitiously day after day in his hunt for a leprechaun, never giving up. 60

It must have been about six months later that Dennis finally got himself a real leprechaun, or so the story goes. You see, I never saw the little fellow myself. Dennis came upon the leprechaun early one evening in the hay in his Uncle Patrick's barn, where he was sleeping peacefully. Dennis grabbed him by the ear and the seat of the pants. 65

The leprechaun let out a screech when Dennis woke him up so rudely like that. And the next thing the leprechaun felt was a very large, rough hand holding his little arm firmly. Looking down at him, shivering with delight, Dennis exclaimed excitedly, "You might as well learn to like being with me, little man, because you're going to stay and support me the rest of my life!" 70

"Don't hurt me!" cried the leprechaun. "I'll do whatever you say! But how can I support you? I'm just a poor fellow." 75

"Poor? You're poor? What's in that little bag there on your hip?"

"Just a few coins, that's all!"

"And what happens when you use them? Tell me that!" demanded Dennis. 80

"When I spend the coins, they're gone, of course!"

"Well, we'll see!" said Dennis as he took a firmer hold of the little man's arm and headed for his favorite pub.

When Dennis walked into the tavern with the leprechaun, you should have seen his friends. You see, all of them had been drinking a good while, so they thought they were seeing things. One of them, who had had a few too many glasses of ale, banged his forehead with the heel of his hand, pushed his empty glass away, and stumbled toward the door. Two others who saw Dennis and the leprechaun started to leave, too, both reciting the "Hail, Mary" as they held on to each other. 85

90

"Wait, fellows!" called Dennis, jerking the leprechaun by the arm roughly. "Your eyes are not playing tricks on you! I've got me a gold mine here, and he's as real as he can be!"

"I have only a few coins!" squealed the leprechaun, helplessly, "but I'll buy you some ale, if you won't hurt me!" 95

Dennis giggled like a schoolgirl who'd just been asked to her first dance, and said, "Now you're talking. Let's see those coins!"

"I'll even sing and dance for you if you won't be so rough with me!" bargained the little man.

100   The news about free drinks and a show made Dennis' friends come back, still not believing their eyes. One of them reached out and patted Dennis on the back as he said haltingly, "I n-never th-thought you'd d-do it, D-Dennis, ol-old boy."

    When the leprechaun dug into his purse with his free hand and held
105 up three gold coins, even the tavernkeeper poured himself a glass of ale. And believe it or not, that little fellow really did sing and dance for them on top of one of the tables. Well, so the story goes. But Dennis still held the leprechaun securely by tightening his belt around the little man and holding the end of it. You see, Dennis wasn't totally ignorant. He had
110 learned well, from his drinking comrades, not to trust anyone.

    So, according to the story, the leprechaun entertained this high-class group for about two hours while they drank their fill and laughed merrily. And it was just as Dennis had said: Every time the leprechaun spent the coins he had in his purse, there were more the next time he
115 opened it.

    Finally, Dennis, his friends, and even the tavernkeeper became sleepy from the many glasses of ale. Dennis, still holding onto the belt, was the last to doze off.

    Just then, schoolmaster McClanahan opened the door of the pub.
120 Seeing the teacher, the leprechaun slipped out of the belt and jumped to the top of the door, right over the schoolmaster's head. Then he stood on his hands on the peak of his hat for a second, kicked his heels playfully in the air, laughed, and disappeared. Of course, Master McClanahan didn't see the leprechaun at all.

125   The schoolmaster walked in and saw the men sleeping. "You drunken bums!" he called in disgust. "Why don't you go home and sleep in your beds?" Slowly, one by one, they raised their heads.

    Then the schoolmaster walked over to Dennis. "Dennis!" he said grabbing him roughly. "Your mother wants you to come home!"
130   "I-I'm h-h-having too m-m-much fun with m-m-my leprechaun, Master McClanahan!" Dennis stammered slowly.

    "Your what?"

    Dennis looked around and saw that the leprechaun was gone. His belt, still in a small circle, was on the table. Dennis was startled almost
135 into being sober.

    "My leprechaun!" said Dennis, still not believing he wasn't there. "My leprechaun with the gold coins! He's gone!"

    "There have been as many leprechauns in this pub tonight as I believe there are in all of Ireland!" said the teacher to Dennis in disgust.
140 "Now, come along with me!"

"He sang for us!" cried Dennis. "He really sang and danced for us and paid for our drinks!"

"Sure he did," said the teacher with a smile, "sure he did. Now let's go. I think the ale has gotten to your brain."

The tavernkeeper had been scared sober a little bit, too, by this time. 145 "He really did bring him in here, Master McClanahan," he said to the teacher. "I saw it with my own eyes. And the little guy paid me with gold coins. Old ones! Not like we use now."

"Where are they?" asked the schoolmaster.

"I put them here in my pocket," replied the tavernkeeper, "because I 150 didn't want to lose them. They looked special."

"Let me see them."

The tavernkeeper dug into his pocket but found nothing but a few coins which he'd had there before. "I don't believe it!" he said, digging deeply into all his pockets, "They were there! They really were there!" 155

"Sure, they were," smiled the teacher; "sure they were."

Dennis got up. Then, leaning on the back of a chair, he said in a loud voice, "Teachers, generally, do a lot of good in a community. But they should stay out of taverns when leprechauns are around. Master Mc-Clanahan here, good man that he is ordinarily, just cheated me out of an 160 easy living!"

"Sure I did," replied the teacher; "sure I did. Now, let's go, Dennis."

A.   A true-or-false quiz on the content of the story.

Mark *T* for the statements which are *true;* mark *F* for the statements which are *false.* Be ready to *give a reason* for your answer in class.

_____ 1. Dennis O'Day received an excellent education.

_____ 2. This story took place when Dennis was still in school.

_____ 3. Dennis did not visit the town library very often.

_____ 4. Miss Reilly had never met Dennis.

_____ 5. Dennis came to the library for a special reason.

_____ 6. Dennis was a slow reader.

_____ 7. The money, which they say each leprechaun has, especially interested Dennis.

_____ **8.** Dennis thought he could live off the money of one leprechaun.

_____ **9.** According to the book Dennis read, leprechauns do not like teachers.

_____ **10.** The book said that teachers in Ireland tell people to be afraid of leprechauns.

_____ **11.** The leprechaun was caught by Dennis in a field.

_____ **12.** The leprechaun which Dennis caught seemed to be worried about being hurt.

_____ **13.** Everybody was happy when Dennis walked into the pub with the leprechaun.

_____ **14.** Dennis was happy when the leprechaun said he would buy them ale.

_____ **15.** Dennis' friends returned when they heard that the leprechaun was going to entertain them.

_____ **16.** The tavernkeeper put a belt around the leprechaun.

_____ **17.** The person who tells the story was there to hear the leprechaun sing and see him dance.

_____ **18.** Master McClanahan did not see the leprechaun, although the leprechaun saw him.

_____ **19.** All the men were asleep when the teacher arrived.

_____ **20.** The men in the pub woke up when the schoolmaster spoke to them.

_____ **21.** Master McClanahan had a drink with Dennis before he took him home.

_____ **22.** The tavernkeeper showed Master McClanahan the gold coins.

_____ **23.** The leprechaun came back while the teacher was there.

_____ **24.** Master McClanahan was Dennis' neighbor.

_____ **25.** The teacher believed Dennis' story about the leprechaun.

B. Vocabulary practice.

1. Underline the best answer.
    a. *Lad* means (lady/lazy man/boy).
    b. *Mischievous* means (annoyingly playful/funny/part spirit and part fairy).
    c. When Dennis said that a leprechaun could support him *the rest of his born days*, he meant that the leprechaun could (buy ale for him and his friends/support him for the remainder of his life/give him all the coins from his purse).
    d. The book Dennis read said that those who have tried to catch a leprechaun have usually *come to grief* in doing so, which means that they (have had a bad experience/have been killed/have been intensely disliked).
    e. To *mutter* means to (speak too loud/speak unclearly in a low voice/speak angrily).
    f. The person who tells the story says that Dennis was not an *ambitious* man, which means in this case that he was not (industrious/lazy/educated).
    g. Dennis *shivered with delight* when he caught the leprechaun, which means that he was (cold/happy/nervous).
    h. When Dennis walked into the pub with the leprechaun, his friends thought they were *seeing things*, which means that they thought (they had had too much to drink/it was time to go home/their minds or eyes were playing tricks on them).
    i. *Ale* is (a type of liquor/anything served in a pub/a type of root beer).
    j. To *giggle* means to (laugh in a silly way/wiggle/squeal).
    k. To *bargain* means to (shout/negotiate/buy).
    l. A *comrade* is a (person who drinks too much/tavern customer/friend).
    m. A *schoolmaster* is (a male schoolteacher/a principal of a school/any teacher in a school).
    n. To *stammer* means to (speak while drunk/speak stumblingly/speak while nervous or afraid).

2. Match the *opposites*.

    a. difficult   1. evil
    b. good   2. late
    c. early   3. easy
    d. rude   4. ignorant
    e. empty   5. full
                        6. kind

3. Match the two-word verbs with words or phrases which mean more or less the *same* (as used in this story).

a. find out	**1.** extend
b. doze off	**2.** learn
c. take off	**3.** remove
d. get up	**4.** surrender
e. set out	**5.** fall asleep
f. give up	**6.** start
	7. arise

C.   Grammar practice.

1. Practice with *adjectives* and *adverbs*. An *adjective* modifies (helps to describe) a noun; an *adverb* modifies (helps to describe) a verb.

In the following sentences, change the *adjective* to an *adverb* to say more or less the same thing.

Examples: He is a <u>slow</u> reader.
He reads <u>slowly</u>.

Dennis was not a <u>good</u> reader.
Dennis did not read <u>well</u>.

They are not <u>ambitious</u> workers.
They do not work <u>ambitiously</u>.

a. They were *slow* in raising their heads.

They raised their heads _____.

b. The leprechaun did not like Dennis' *rough* treatment.

The leprechaun did not like it when Dennis treated him

_____.

c. It was *easy* for him to read the paragraph in two minutes.

He read the paragraph _____ in two minutes.

d. With a *quick* grab, he caught him.

He caught him by grabbing him _____.

e. He set out on a *serious* hunt for a leprechaun.

He started to hunt _____ for a leprechaun.

f. Did he have a *firm* hold on the little fellow?

Did he hold the little fellow _____?

g. The little man gave out a *helpless* squeal.

The little man squealed _____.

   h. The speech of the men was halting.

     The men spoke _____.

   i. Leprechauns are *good* singers and dancers.

     Leprechauns sing and dance _____.

   j. I had a *secure* hold on him with my long belt tightened around his waist.

     I held him _____ by tightening my long belt around his waist.

Change in these sentences the *adverb* to an *adjective*.

Examples: I turned the wheel *quickly.*
          I gave the wheel a *quick* turn.

          She spoke *softly.*
          She spoke in a *soft* voice.

   k. Jane and Joan study *seriously.*

     Jane and Joan are _____ students.

   l. The boys drive *well.*

     The boys are _____ drivers.

   m. Some of the students speak *slowly.*

     Some of the students are _____ speakers.

   n. The director visits our classes *frequently.*

     The director is a _____ visitor to our classes.

   o. They worked *hard* when they were here.

     They were _____ workers when they were here.

   p. I'm sure they worked *ambitiously* on that project.

     I'm sure they were _____ workers on that project.

   q. The student whispered *hoarsely* to his friend in the next row.
     The student spoke to his friend in the next row in a

     _____ whisper.

   r. Miss Harkins explains things *well.*

     Miss Harkins is _____ at explaining things.

    s. She smiled at us *pleasantly* when she greeted us.

       When she greeted us, she had a _____ smile on her face.

    t. In this state, twenty-one is the age for drinking *legally*.

       Twenty-one is the age for _____ drinking in this state.

2. Practice with pronouns.

Subject pronouns identify the *subject* in a sentence.
Object pronouns identify the *object* of a verb.

Subject pronouns	Object pronouns
I	me
you	you
he	him
she	her
it	it
we	us
you (plural)	you (plural)
they	them

Examples: *He* learned to read.
            Someone taught *him* to read.

            I need help with this.
            Can you help *me*?

            My brother can speak English better than *I*.
            His friend helped *him* learn.

Choose the pronoun which will correctly complete the sentence.

    a. (He/Him) sat in the pub all day.
    b. Was someone trying to talk to (he/him)?
    c. Miss Reilly knows more than (we/us) do.
    d. (She/Her) and the teacher were looking for Dennis.
    e. Is Dennis more ambitious than (they/them) are?
    f. (We/Us) and our friends helped Dennis look for the leprechaun.
    g. (He/Him) and Norman did not believe Dennis.
    h. (She/Her) and another librarian helped Dennis find out about leprechauns.
    i. Dennis thanked (she/her) very much.
    j. My brother and (I/me) went with Dennis.

    k. Dennis thanked (I/me), too, for helping.

    l. Did the teacher know more than (they/them) did?

    m. The teachers tell (they/them) not to believe in leprechauns.

D. Questions for discussion.

    1. What type of person do you think is telling this story? Explain.

    2. Why do you suppose the storyteller adds things like "so the story goes" and "according to the story" when he speaks of the leprechaun?

    3. Why did Dennis use his fingers and move his lips as he read? Why is it a disadvantage when you have to read that way?

    4. Why did the men in the tavern react as they did when Dennis came in with the leprechaun? Why do you suppose the two said the "Hail, Mary" as they started to leave the tavern?

    5. What did the teacher mean when he said that he thought the ale had *gotten to Dennis' brain?*

    6. Do you think Dennis had told his drinking comrades about his hunt for the leprechaun? Why or why not? Do you think he had told his mother or Master McClanahan? Why or why not?

E. Writing practice or more discussion.

    1. Write a paragraph (or tell the class) about what kind of a person Dennis was.

    2. Look up something on leprechauns. Then write a paragraph (or tell the class) about what you have learned.

    3. Write a paragraph (or tell the class) about mythical people or creatures which some people in your country believe are real.

    4. Write a paragraph (or tell the class) about why educated people usually are not believers in such creatures as leprechauns.

    5. Write a paragraph (or tell the class) about ways in which some people, like Dennis, work harder at trying to *get rich quickly* than they do at a regular job.

F. A bit of humor.

Near where Dennis lived, there was a single girl named Fiona, about twenty-five, being visited one evening by a single man named Paedar, who was about thirty. Now, in those parts at that time, when a girl got to be twenty-five and was not married she started getting a little worried, if you know what I mean. And a single man of thirty was just about getting equally nervous about maybe spending his life alone. But Paedar was not great at expressing himself.

Now, this single man, who had been farming all alone for a few years, was doing his best to try to bring his five-year relationship with Fiona to a head, as the two sat together on the porch swing at her house.

"Fiona?" he said, moving a little closer to her.

"Yes, Paedar?" she said with a smile.

"Fiona, I uh—that is—uh—you—I have this place, and—uh— well . . ."

"Yes, Paedar?"

"Well, you see, I have this piece of land and—uh—I—even have a little house, and I thought maybe you . . ."

About this time the girl's mother noticed it was getting a little dark for her daughter to be out there alone with that fellow, so she called, "Fiona, is Paedar there, yet?"

Fiona smiled as she looked into Paedar's eyes and called back to her mother, "No, mom, but he's getting there!"

Was It a Dream?

A story by Guy de Maupassant (adapted for ESL).

I loved her madly! I met her and lived every day on her tenderness, her beauty, her love. I was so wrapped up in everything about her that I no longer cared whether it was day or night, winter or summer, on this old earth of ours.

5   And then she died. How? I do not know. I no longer know anything. She came home one evening in the rain. She coughed, then had a high fever. There were doctors. There was medicine. I don't remember anything! I have forgotten everything! Everything! Everything! She's gone. They put her in a coffin! The sound of the hammer that nailed the

10 coffin shut is still pounding in my head! She's buried in the ground! I don't believe it!

    After the funeral, I couldn't face the walls where we had lived. I couldn't face my friends. The next morning I left Paris.

    Yesterday I returned to take up my life again. But when I saw the

15 rooms where we had lived and loved, I was seized by a new attack of grief. I had to leave that place again.

    As I left weeping, I stopped in front of a full-length mirror in the hallway—a mirror which I placed there for her. How often she stood there admiring herself! And I, standing near her, admired her much

20 more than she admired herself!

    "Surely this glass contains some of her reflection," I thought. Then I touched it. "It's cold," I wept. Oh, what torments seize a man when he has loved and lost!

152

I wandered into the street. Without thinking, I went to the cemetery. I found her simple grave. It had a white marble cross with these few 25 words:

SHE LOVED, WAS LOVED, AND DIED.

"How horrible to think that she is below here!" I cried, "that beautiful body and pretty face, *decayed*!"

I wept there and didn't want to leave. Then I was seized by a mad 30 wish—to spend the night there. I hid so they would not find me when they closed for the night. Then it began to grow dark. "Clank! Clank!" The gates were closed. I was alone, perfectly alone.

When it was quite dark I left the place where I had been hiding. I began to walk softly, slowly, quietly through that place full of dead 35 people. Then I tried to find her grave again but could not.

I felt my way around, madly knocking against the tombs with my hands, my feet, my knees, my chest, even with my head! But I was unable to find her. I groped like a blind man on a windy day. I felt the stones, the crosses, the iron railings, the wreaths and faded flowers! 40

Graves! Graves! Graves! Nothing but graves! I was frightened as I floundered in those narrow rows between them. I tried to read the names with my fingers, for in the blackness my eyes were of no use. There was no moon! It was so dark!

I sat down. "Why am I here," I asked, "the one living person in this 45 place of the dead?" I could hear my heart beat. Then I heard something else. What was it? It seemed that the slab of marble on which I was sitting was moving! It *was* moving—rising! I got up as fast as I could. Then I saw a naked skeleton arise from the grave and read aloud in an eerie voice what was engraved on the stone: "Here lies Jacques Olivant, 50 who died at the age of fifty-one. He loved his family, was kind and honorable, and died in the grace of the Lord."

Then I heard this body of bones give out a cry of anguish as he took a stone from the path and scratched out the engraving he had just read. He then took the tip of the bone that had been his forefinger and wrote 55 in luminous letters,

HERE LIES JACQUES OLIVANT, WHO DIED AT THE AGE OF FIFTY-ONE. HE HASTENED HIS FATHER'S DEATH WITH HIS UNKINDNESS BECAUSE HE WANTED HIS MONEY. HE WAS CRUEL TO HIS WIFE AND CHILDREN. HE DECEIVED HIS NEIGHBORS, ROBBED EVERYONE HE COULD, AND DIED A 60 MISERABLE MAN.

When the skeleton finished writing, he looked at what he had written. He seemed satisfied that he had finally done an honest thing! Then I heard the moving of stone slabs and rattling of bones all around me.
65 Other graves were being opened and others were writing the truth about themselves on their gravestones. I saw that many of them had been malicious, dishonest, and jealous. I saw them write how they had hated, stolen, cheated, and lied—these good fathers, faithful wives, devoted sons, and pure daughters!

70 I was amazed at what I saw! Then I thought, "Surely, she too, is writing! I must see what the love of my life is writing!"

I ran without fear past the half-open coffins, the corpses, and the skeletons. I found her and recognized her once-beautiful face. As I got there she was scratching out SHE LOVED, WAS LOVED, AND
75 DIED. Then she took the bone of her finger and wrote,

HAVING GONE OUT IN THE RAIN ONE DAY IN ORDER TO DECEIVE HER LOVER, SHE CAUGHT COLD AND DIED.

They found me at daybreak, lying on the grave, unconscious.

A. Questions on the content of the story.

1. Who tells the story?
2. About whom is he speaking at the beginning of the story?
3. What happened to the woman he loved?
4. In which city does this story take place?
5. Why did he leave the city?
6. Why did he return?
7. Describe the woman's grave.
8. When he was visiting the cemetery, what did he decide to do?
9. Why did he *hide* in the cemetery?
10. Why did he have a problem finding his way in the cemetery after he came out from his hiding place? Why was it especially dark that night?
11. Since he could not see, how did he try to read the names on the gravestones?
12. Where did he sit down?
13. How did the skeleton remove the words on the gravestone?
14. What did the skeleton use to write the new words?
15. What did this man hear after this first skeleton came out and changed the message on his gravestone?

16. Why did he try again to find the grave of the woman he loved?
17. Did he leave the cemetery when he saw what she wrote on her gravestone? Explain.

B.   Vocabulary practice.

1. Underline the best answer.
    a. This man says that he loved this woman *madly*, which means that (he loved her very much/he loved her but was angry with her/he loved her, although she was insane).
    b. He says he was *wrapped up* in everything about her, which means that (he could think about nothing but her/he couldn't tell winter from summer/he constantly brought her beautiful gifts).
    c. A *coffin* is (a grave/a cemetery/a casket).
    d. To *weep* means to (cry/mourn/seize).
    e. He said he couldn't *face the walls* where they had lived, which means that (he couldn't look at the walls/he couldn't stand being in the place where they had lived/he wanted to redecorate the apartment).
    f. A *full-length mirror* is one which (is from floor to ceiling/covers the entire wall/is the right size for a person to see himself or herself from head to foot).
    g. This man says that *torments* seize men who have loved and lost, which means that they (suffer in the mind/suffer in the body/weep).
    h. To *decay* means to (decompose/die/bury).
    i. To *grope* means to (be blind/be in the dark/reach out blindly).
    j. To *flounder* means to (stumble/catch a fish/find one's way).
    k. An *eerie* voice is a voice which sounds (wierd/high pitched/ unclear).
    l. A cry of *anguish* is a cry of (sadness/distress/happiness).
    m. *Luminous* means (dark/large/able to be seen in the dark).
    n. To *hasten* means to (kill/hurry/harm).
    o. *Miserable* means (wretched/happy/sad).
    p. *Malicious* means (very harmful/delicious/jealous).
    q. A *corpse* is (a grave/the body of a dead person/a group of people).
    r. To *deceive* means to (be unfaithful/catch cold/cheat).

2. Match the *opposites.*

a. remember	**1.** leave
b. die	**2.** begin
c. return	**3.** finish
d. find	**4.** open
e. close	**5.** forget
f. start	**6.** live
	7. lose

C.   Grammar practice.

   1. Write the correct form of the verb (look, for example, for indication of tense).

     a. When she was alive, he _____ to be
                      (want)
     with her all the time.

     b. He couldn't _____ her.
                   (forget)

     c. She was _____ in that cemetery.
                (bury)

     d. He was _____ to hide when I saw him.
                (try)

     e. The woman was _____ by him.
                (love)

     f. When he thought of her, he _____.
                    (weep)

     g. He was so sad that he had to leave the place where they
     had _____.
           (live)

     h. When he saw her grave, an attack of grief _____
                             (seize)
     him.

     i. She had _____ in front of that mirror
                (stand)
     many times.

     j. Was she _____ by that man?
                (admire)

k. I don't think he had ever _____ a
(lost)

loved one before.

l. I think he did _____ to spend the
(want)

night there.

m. His heart was _____ very fast.
(beat)

n. Jacques Olivant had _____ when he
(die)

was only fifty-one years old.

o. After he wrote the words, he _____
(cry)

out in a loud voice.

2. Practice with *adjectives* and *adverbs.*

An *adjective* helps to describe a *noun.*

Examples: His love for her was *tender.*
His movements were *slow.*
She is a *good* teacher.

An *adverb* helps to describe a *verb.*

Examples: He loved her *tenderly.*
He moved *slowly.*
She teaches *well.*

a. In the following sentences, change the *adjective* to an
adverb.

Examples: His admiration for her was *great.*
He admired her *greatly.*

He walked with *soft* steps.
He stepped *softly* as he walked.

(1) He groped like a *blind* man as he walked.

He groped _____ as he walked.
(2) The rising of the grave slab was *slow.*

The grave slab rose _____.
(3) They are *honest* in their business dealings.

They deal in business _____.

(4) My movements were *quiet* as I walked.

I moved _____ as I walked.

(5) I think this man was *mad* in his love for her.

I think this man loved her _____.

b. In the following sentences, change the *adverb* to an *adjective*.

Example: He treated his friends *honorably*.
He was *honorable* in his treatment of his friends.

(1) They spoke *quietly*.

They were _____ when they spoke.

(2) The grave opened *slowly*.

The opening of the grave was _____.

(3) Skeletons write *well*.

Skeletons are _____ writers.

(4) I watched the skeleton *nervously*.

I was _____ as I watched the skeleton.

(5) They treated their father *maliciously*.

They were _____ in their treatment of their father.

D. Questions for discussion (in small groups, if possible).

1. What do you think of the man's love for the woman? Explain. Do you think she had the same feeling for him? Explain. Do you think they were married? Explain.

2. What do you think of the man's grief? Explain. Do you think *she* would have grieved like this if *he* had died?

3. Do you think it is a good idea to visit the grave of a loved one who has died? Explain. Do you think it would be a good idea to stay in the cemetery *at night*? Explain.

4. What inscription on *her* gravestone do you think he expected her to write? Explain.

5. What kinds of inscriptions, or epitaphs, if any, do they write on gravestones in your country? Are there any special *customs* regarding the marking of graves in your culture?

6. If the dead people everywhere in the world would write the truth about themselves, do you think many friends and loved ones would be surprised at what they would see? Explain.

E.   Writing practice (or more discussion).

1. Write a paragraph describing (or speak to the group about) *this man.* (Include what you imagine to be his *age, appearance, vocation, personality,* and so on.

2. Write a paragraph describing (or speak to the group about) *the woman* whom this man loved so madly. (Again, use your imagination.)

3. Write a paragraph (or speak to the group) about what this man did to try to overcome his grief compared to *what you think a person should do* to overcome grief.

4. Write a paragraph (or speak to the group) about whether you think this story or a part of it was, in fact *real* or a *dream.* Explain.

F.   Reading practice.

Practice reading aloud the first two paragraphs of the story. Try to read it *as though you were this man.*

G.   A bit of humor.

One day a boy, about twelve, had to stay after school because he had misbehaved in the classroom. He was already late for delivering his news-papers, so he ran out of the door of the school when he was allowed to leave.

Although it was almost dark, he decided to take a shortcut through a cemetery on his way home. Halfway through, he stumbled on an old gravestone and fell to the ground.

As the boy got up, he heard music. In fact, it sounded like piano music was coming out of one of the graves. He walked slowly and cautiously toward the sound. There, under the gravestone of a famous composer of music who was buried there, he saw light through a small crack.

Bending down, he peeked through and saw, in the grave, a man play-ing a piano. As the boy watched, he noticed that the musician would play a little and then erase some of the notes on the page in front of him. Then he would play a little more and again erase more notes.

The boy's curiosity, by this time had become greater than his fear, so he called, "Mister?"

The musician looked up at him and said in a wierd-sounding voice, "Yes?"

"What are you doing?" he asked.

The musician took up his eraser again and said, "Decomposing, of course."

The Loving Mother

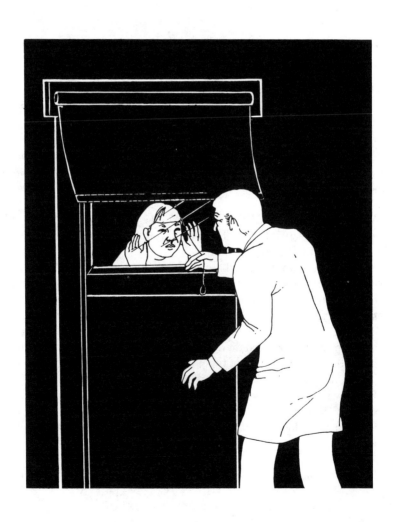

Based on a story told by a student from the Island of Hokkaido, Japan.

Shoji Sakota was a pharmacist in the city of Sapporo on Hokkaido Island in northern Japan. He lived alone in a small apartment behind the drugstore, for his wife had died several years earlier. Because he lived there in the same building, he sometimes worked in the pharmacy after it was closed. 5

One stormy winter night in 1964, he closed the shop at the end of the day and began working on his record books at his small desk in the rear of the store. He worked quite late because it was close to the end of the year, the time when he had to prepare his annual business report. The only light on in the entire store was over the little desk where he was 10 working.

At about midnight there was a knock on the door. "Who could that be?" he said to himself. "Surely whoever it is can see that the store is closed." Ignoring the knock, he went back to his work.

Then he heard something again. He looked toward the door but 15 thought this time that the noise was perhaps caused by the wind. Again he continued with his record books.

A third time he heard the noise. This time it was louder and definitely sounded like a person knocking.

"Maybe it's an emergency," he said aloud, as he started toward the 20 door. He lifted the shade which was pulled down over the window of the door, turned on the outside light, and looked out. He was surprised to see a young woman standing there who appeared to be quite nervous.

Thinking that perhaps it was some kind of trick to rob him, he did not
25 unlock the door. Instead, he called out, "The store is closed! It will open
again at eight o'clock in the morning!" Then he let the shade down
again.

"Please, sir," she called in a pleading voice, "I need something for my
baby." As he lifted the shade again, she called, "I beg you to help me,
30 sir!" He saw this time that she was pleading with her hands and body as
well as with her voice.

Feeling confident that it was indeed an emergency, the pharmacist
opened the door to let her in. She entered and stood in front of him with
her head bent down. Mr. Sakota noticed that the woman was very
35 thin—too thin—and that her skin seemed abnormally light. Her long,
black hair hung in a disheveled mass around her head and shoulders,
and her simple kimono seemed like it had been worn to bed.

"What can I do for you?" he asked sympathetically, feeling certain
that the woman's baby was very ill, perhaps dying. As she raised her
40 head Mr. Sakota was quite startled, for her eyes seemed to be looking
through him, not at him.

"I need amé* on a stick for my baby," she said softly.

"Amé?" he asked in surprise, for he thought she needed medicine for
a serious illness.

45 "Yes, sir," she said again in a thin, soft voice, "my baby likes amé."

The pharmacist put the amé on a stick for her. She paid the few cents
for it, thanked him kindly, and went out quickly into the stormy night.

"How strange!" thought Mr. Sakota to himself, "Amé on a stick! What
a strange request in the night!" He shook his head and went back to his
50 work.

In a few minutes he decided to quit working for the night, for he
was tired and for some reason couldn't get the image of the strange
visitor out of his mind. "What a mysterious-looking woman!" he said to
himself as he turned out his light and went to his apartment. "Those
55 *eyes*, especially! They look like they belong to someone from another
world!"

The next two nights the same thing happened. Mr. Sakota was in the
store till past midnight, again working on his report. The same woman
came each of those nights, at about the same time, for the same thing:
60 amé on a stick. She looked and spoke the same, too, and each night she
hurried out after receiving the amé. Her appearance and her request

---

*Amé (ahmaý) is a nutritious type of Japanese candy used for pacifying young children.

were so mysterious to Mr. Sakota that he forgot to ask her why she came at midnight rather than during the day when the shop was open.

After she came the third night, the pharmacist asked a photographer friend of his to hide in the store and take pictures of her so he could study her appearance. 65

She did, in fact, come the fourth night, looking the same, making the identical request, and hurrying away again into the cold night.

Mr. Sakota was pleased that this time a number of pictures of her were taken by his friend—until they developed the film! To their great surprise, the pictures clearly showed objects in the store but *not the woman*! It was as if she had not been there at all! "I saw her through the lens of the camera!" exclaimed Mr. Sakota's friend. "She looked exactly as you had described!" 70

"How strange!" said the pharmacist as he stroked his small beard. "How very strange!" 75

They told no one, but decided that if she would come again, they would follow her to see if they could find out something about her.

She did come again the next night, at the same time, with the same request. And after purchasing amé she again left quickly. This time, however, Mr. Sakota and his friend followed her, as she almost seemed to float down the street in the cold night air. 80

Since they were not skilled at this kind of thing, the men were easily noticed by the woman, but it didn't seem to matter to her that they were following. In fact, after a minute, she acted almost as though she wanted them to see where she was going. 85

A few blocks away, she turned down a narrow side street and walked up three flights of stairs in an old apartment building and disappeared through a door at the end of a dark, narrow hallway. The men followed, just a little behind. Seeing that the door of the apartment was left open, they walked in. It was dark, but they soon found the light switch. 90

There, in a bed, they saw a baby, perhaps eight or nine months old, licking amé on a stick. The child seemed to be happy, satisfied, and well. A young woman lay beside him, appearing to be asleep.

"It's the same woman!" whispered Mr. Sakota's friend, "but how could she have gone to sleep so fast?" 95

Thinking perhaps that she was just *acting* as though she were sleeping, Mr. Sakota walked over and touched her on the shoulder. She didn't stir. Then he looked closer and put his hand on her bare neck. "Her body is lifeless and cold!" he exclaimed in a whisper. "She's dead!" 100

Then the pharmacist looked a little more closely and said, "In fact, she's been dead for a number of days!"

A.   Questions on the content of the story.

1. In what part of Japan did Shoji Sakota live?
2. Where was the apartment in which he lived?
3. How long ago did this story take place?
4. Why was he working late?
5. Why didn't Mr. Sakota go to the door when he heard the knock the first time?
6. Why didn't he want to open the door when he saw the woman through the window of the door?
7. Why did he finally let her in?
8. What did the woman ask for? Why did this request surprise the pharmacist?
9. Why did Mr. Sakota decide to quit working for the night a few minutes after the woman left the store?
10. How many more times did she come before he asked his friend to take pictures of her?
11. Why did Mr. Sakota want the pictures taken?
12. What did the film show when it was developed?
13. How many people did Mr. Sakota and his photographer friend tell about this?
14. What did they do the next time she came?
15. What did the woman do when she noticed that Mr. Sakota and his friend were following her?
16. Where did she lead them?
17. Whom did the men find in the woman's small apartment?
18. How sick was the baby?
19. What did they think at first when they saw the woman in the bed?
20. How long did the pharmacist think she had been dead?

B.   Vocabulary practice.

1. Underline the best answer.
    a. A *pharmacist* is (a person who prepares medicines/a drug addict/a drugstore owner).
    b. *Annual* means (end of the year/yearly/monthly)
    c. To *ignore* means to (be an ignorant person/refuse to take notice of/make a knocking noise).
    d. The pharmacist thought that maybe it was an *emergency*, which means that he thought (someone wanted to talk to

him/someone wanted him to make a house call/someone needed some medicine immediately).
  e. To *beg* means to (ask/call/plead).
  f. The woman's hair hung in a *disheveled* mass, which means that it was (not clean/not arranged/not pretty).
  g. *Illness* means (sickness/seriousness/emergency).
  h. He decided to *quit* working for the night, which means that he decided to (stop working/work more quietly/go to bed).
  i. To *hurry* means to do something (quickly/quietly/strangely).
  j. Mr. Sakota's friend said that the woman looked *exactly* as he described, which means that she looked (strange/ mysterious/the same).
  k. It didn't seem *to matter* to the woman that the men were following her, which means that she didn't (mind/act strange/follow them).
  l. When Mr. Sakota touched the woman on the shoulder, she didn't *stir*, which means that she didn't (sleep/ move/get up).
  m. *Lifeless* means (lively/alive/without life).
2. Match the *opposites*.

   a. begin   1. lower
   b. close   2. leave
   c. purchase   3. start
   d. lift   4. open
   e. enter   5. sell
   f. follow   6. lead
                     7. finish

3. Write a sentence with each of these words. (*Do not* use ideas from the story.)

   a. _____ ignored _____

   b. _____ knocked _____

   c. _____ appeared _____

   d. _____ pleaded _____

   e. _____ followed _____

C.   Questions for discussion.

1. If you had been Mr. Sakota, do you think you would have been afraid to let this woman in at midnight? Explain.
2. If Mr. Sakota had asked the woman why she came at midnight, what do you think she would have answered?
3. What do you think Mr. Sakota meant when he said the woman's eyes looked like they belonged to someone from another world?
4. Do you think taking a picture of the woman was a good idea? Explain.
5. What would *you* have thought if you had taken pictures of this woman and she did not appear on them when the film was developed?
6. Do you think something like this could really happen? Explain.

D.   Writing practice.

1. Imagine that you are Mr. Sakota and that you keep a *diary* or *journal* of things that happen each day and of your thoughts concerning those things.
   a. Write an entry in your diary for the first night the girl appeared.
   b. Write an entry in your diary for the night when you and your photographer friend developed the film.
   c. Write an entry for the night you found the woman in her apartment with her baby.
2. Write a paragraph about this woman (who you think she was, whether you think she had friends, how you think she died, why she was not found for days, and so on).
3. Write a short article *for the newspaper,* imagining that you have just interviewed Mr. Sakota and his friend as well as the police and doctor who were called to the scene by Mr. Sakota.
4. If you have heard of a situation somewhat similar to this in your country, write a paragraph telling about it.
5. Write a conversation between Mr. Sakota and a medical doctor who is a friend of his, which takes place the day after he and the photographer found the woman and her baby.

E. A bit of humor.

A writer was spending the night in a house that people said was haunted. Since he didn't believe in ghosts, he went to sleep without fear.

Suddenly he was awakened by the feeling that someone was in the room with him. He lit his cigarette lighter and saw someone standing at the foot of the bed.

"Who are you?" he asked.

"A ghost," the person replied.

"I don't believe in ghosts."

"Well, you'd better change your mind. I'm as real as you are, only my existence is different."

"If you're real, how about letting me take your picture?"

"I'll let you," replied the ghost, "but under one condition, and that is, that you take only *one*."

The writer reached for the light switch.

"Don't do that! If you turn on a light, I'm going to leave."

The writer groped for his camera and finally got the flash attachment on. How he was wishing that he had gotten some new batteries, since he had no supporting light in the room! Finally he was ready.

"I'm right here at the foot of the bed and I'm even smiling. But, remember now, only *one* picture."

The writer clicked the camera. Immediately after he took the picture a cool breeze went by his face and the ghost was gone.

When the film was developed, there was nothing on it but blackness, however. So the writer concluded that the spirit was willing, but the flash was weak.

Life in Death

*Based on "The Oval Portrait" by Edgar Allan Poe.**

The painter was known for his ability to put life on canvas like no other artist of his time. His skills in the use of colors and hues was so great that some who viewed the paintings he created said that they were more true to life than life itself.

He, indeed, was a skilled artist. When he painted fruit, it seemed as though you could take it from the picture and eat it. When he put a field of spring flowers on canvas, you could view the scene in the painting and imagine yourself walking in that field, feeling a gentle breeze carrying the fragrance of the flowers. And when he put a face on his canvas with his brush, it looked like a person of flesh and blood with life and breath.

One day this skilled artist met a beautiful woman who immediately became the object of his affections. As he observed her and spoke with her, he admired her more and more. He showered her with kindness and words of praise until she consented to be his wife.

Not long after they were married, however, the beautiful woman found out that she was more the object of his artistic interest than of his affections. When he admired her classic beauty, it was as though he were standing in front of a work of art rather than in front of a human being to whom he had pledged his love and promised his life. And soon he expressed his great desire to put her rare beauty on canvas.

*Edgar Allan Poe (1809–1849) lived and wrote, during his short life, in several eastern cities of the United States. "Life in Death," published in 1842, was later published under the name "The Oval Portrait."

"Please sit for me in the studio," he pleaded, "and I will immortalize your beauty. The work will be my masterpiece!"

She was humble and obedient as well as flattered by his words, so she said, "Yes, my love. I will be happy to pose for you."

25   So the beautiful, young wife of the artist sat meekly for hours in his studio, not complaining. Day after day she sat obediently, smiling as she posed, because she loved him and because she hoped that he would see her love in her smile and obedience.

She sometimes wanted to call out to him, "Please love me and want
30   me as a *person* rather than as an object!" But, instead, she spoke nothing but words which pleased him.

Once, as she lay sleepless in bed at night, she planned to say to him the next day, "My dear husband, I am jealous of your mistress!" She thought that surely he would answer in surprise. "Mistress? I have no
35   one but you!" And then she would say, "Your mistress is *your art!*" However, somehow she was never courageous enough to say any of the words, so she continued to sit for him patiently, hour after hour, day after day, week after week. Her love for him gave her the patience, for she knew how much pleasure he took in this task.

40   The artist was a passionate, wild, and moody man who became so involved in his work that he saw only what he wanted to see. He did not, or could not, see, as she smiled on, that she was becoming weak and dispirited. He did not, or could not, see that though the flesh tones were fresh and beautiful on his canvas, the color was leaving the face of
45   his lovely model.

At length, as the labor drew nearer to its conclusion, the painter became wilder in his passion for his work. He only rarely turned his eyes from the canvas to look at his wife, though she continued to sit patiently for him. If he had looked at her more often and more carefully,
50   he would have noticed that the tints which he so skillfully spread on the canvas were drawn from her cheeks and the smile was taken from her lips.

Finally, after weeks passed, he surveyed his work for the finishing touches. A brush needed to be touched lightly to the mouth, and a tint
55   needed to be added carefully to the eye.

Since the woman knew that he had almost completed the task, her spirits were revived momentarily. Then, when the brush was given and the tint placed, the painter stood back, enthralled by what he had placed on the canvas with the skill of his hand and mind!

60   As he stood there gazing at his beautiful work of art, he cried with a

loud voice, "This is indeed *life* itself!" Then he turned to his beloved and saw that *she was dead!*

A. A true-or-false quiz on the content of the story. Mark *T* for the statements which are *true* and *F* for those which are *false*. Be ready in class to give a reason for your answer.

_____ 1. The special skill of this artist was in painting *life*.

_____ 2. His skill in painting life was almost as great as that of other artists in those days.

_____ 3. Everything this artist painted looked real.

_____ 4. The artist persuaded a professional model to marry him.

_____ 5. The woman saw, before they were married, that he admired her beauty more than he loved her.

_____ 6. The woman persuaded the artist to paint her portrait.

_____ 7. The artist wanted his portrait of her to be the best work of art he ever created.

_____ 8. The woman complained to her husband occasionally, but he wouldn't listen.

_____ 9. The woman smiled as she posed obediently because she thought that in this way she might win his love.

_____ 10. The woman had a great desire to plead with him to love her.

_____ 11. She spoke to him in bed one night about her feeling of jealousy.

_____ 12. The fact that the woman loved the artist helped her to do what he wanted.

_____ 13. The painter was a patient and understanding man.

_____ 14. The artist realized that the woman was becoming weak and dispirited.

_____ 15. When he was finishing his work, he looked at her more often and more carefully.

_____ 16. It took the artist a number of weeks to finish this portrait of his wife.

_____ 17. The woman became a little stronger for a short time when she realized that he was almost finished with the portrait.

_____ 18. The artist did not notice what was happening to his wife while he was putting her beauty on canvas.

_____ 19. Even in the end, the woman said nothing about how she felt.

_____ 20. The woman was excited and pleased with the completed work of art.

B. Vocabulary practice.

1. Underline the best answer.
   a. *Skill* is more or less the same as (creativity/love/ability).
   b. To *view* means to (look at/look for/look up).
   c. *Affection* means (artistic interest/fondness/thought).
   d. The beautiful woman became the *object of the artist's affections*, which means that (she was the center of his attention and love/he objected to her/he thought of her only as an object).
   e. To *consent* means to (disagree/agree/love).
   f. To *admire* means to (disregard/love/think highly of).
   g. To *observe* means to (watch/praise/serve).
   h. To *immortalize* means to (give a moral life/give a life without ending/give life).
   i. A *masterpiece* is (a piece of artistic work/an extraordinary artistic achievement/a beautiful painting).
   j. To *flatter* means to (praise excessively/make flat/love greatly).
   k. The woman *posed* for the artist, which means that (she was obedient/she smiled hour after hour/she stayed in the position the artist wanted so that he could paint her portrait).
   l. *Sleepless* means (without sleep/sleepy/asleep).
   m. To be *jealous* means to be (loving/patient/envious).
   n. When the woman referred to his art as *his mistress*, she meant that (he loved his art more than he loved her/he was a wild and moody man/he was a dedicated artist).

     o. *Task* means (masterpiece/work of art/job).

     p. To be *dispirited* is to be (without patience/without enthusiasm/without hope).

     q. To *survey* means to (look over/look up/look for).

     r. To *revive* means to (bring back to life/be dispirited/die).

     s. The painter was *enthralled* by what he saw, which means that (he was held spellbound/he stood back/he was somewhat satisfied).

2. Match the *opposites*.

a. create	**1.** disagree
b. love	**2.** enter
c. consent	**3.** destroy
d. finish	**4.** hate
e. leave	**5.** begin
f. add	**6.** admire
	7. take away

3. Form an opposite by adding the prefix, *dis-*.

Example: agree   disagree

Form an opposite by adding the prefix *dis- to those words which may be formed in this manner.* Leave the others blank.

     a. continue _____

     b. obey _____

     c. promise _____

     d. admire _____

     e. please _____

     f. appear _____

C. Grammar practice.

     1. Write the correct form of the verb (looking for indications in the sentence of tense, for example).

          a. That painter is _____ by everyone.
                        (know)

          b. He has _____ many portraits.
                  (paint)

c. Does it _____ to you that his work is
(seem)
good?

d. When we visited him, he was _____
(work)
on his masterpiece.

e. Have all his works of art _____ good?
(be)

f. The woman thought at first that she was _____
(love)
by him.

g. She soon _____ out that he loved her
(find)
beauty more than he loved her.

h. When he sees a pretty woman, he _____
(want)
to paint her portrait.

i. After they were _____, she posed for
(marry)
him.

j. She sat hour after hour and never _____.
(complain)

k. She tried to think of what to say to him as she

_____ in bed at night.
(lie)

l. The artist was so _____ in his work
(involve)
that he did not look at her.

m. She knew that he was _____ a lot of
(take)
pleasure in his work.

n. When he is so involved in a work of art, he doesn't

_____ anything else.
(notice)

    o. As she sits there, she _____ that he
                            (hope)

    will notice her.

    p. The masterpiece was _____ by the
                           (survey)

    artist.

    q. After the painting had been _____ by
                            (touch)

    the brush once more, it was finished.

    r. Didn't he _____ what was happening
                    (see)

    to her?

    s. It seemed as though the color on the canvas was

    _____ from her cheeks.
     (draw)

    t. Didn't he notice that she had _____?
                             (die)

2. Write a sentence using these verb forms. (*Do not* use ideas from the story.)

    a. _____ knows _____

    b. _____ knew _____

    c. _____ known _____

    d. _____ meet _____

    e. _____ meets _____

    f. _____ met _____

    g. _____ speaks _____

    h. _____ spoke _____

    i. _____ speaking _____

    j. _____ spoken _____

D. Questions for discussion.

    1. What do you think people meant when they said that this artist's paintings were *more true to life than life itself?*

2. Do you like paintings which make things look *true to life?* Explain.

3. Do you think that the artist *truly loved* the woman when he showered her with kindness and words of praise, before they were married?

4. How do you think the woman *found out* that she was more the object of his artistic interest than of his affections?

5. Do you think that a beautiful woman *in your country* would pose obediently for her artist husband? Explain.

6. Do you think *you* would have the courage to say something to your husband *if you were this woman?* Explain.

7. In what circumstance has someone you know been able to *see only* what he or she *wanted* to see? Have you been in such a circumstance? Explain.

8. Do you think it's possible for a person to become *so involved in work* that he or she does not notice what is happening to his or her loved ones? Explain.

E. Writing practice (or more discussion).

1. Write a paragraph describing (or describe to the class) *the painter, the woman,* or both.

2. Write a paragraph explaining (or tell the class) what you think this woman should have done to try to make the artist realize what he was doing? (Remember that he was a *passionate, wild,* and *moody* man and that she *loved* him.)

3. Write the conversation between the woman and the artist which she was starting to imagine and plan as she lay sleepless in her bed. (Have each person speak at least four or five times.)

4. Write a paragraph (or tell the class) about the *irony* of this artist's desire to *immortalize* his wife's beauty.

5. Write a paragraph (or tell the class) about whether or not you think a person can actually die from lack of attention and affection. Give an example if you can.

6. Write a paragraph (or tell the class) about a similar story or incident you have heard or read about.

F. A bit of humor.

Some years ago there lived a rich man who loved sports cars and spent a great deal of money collecting them. He loved these cars so much that he wrote in his will that he wanted to be buried in one of them when he died.

Years passed, and he did, in fact, die. In accordance with his will, a grave was dug large enough for one of his finest cars. Then his body was propped up in the driver's seat of this beautiful car for the burial.

After the funeral service, the car and its "driver" were lowered into the grave, and the mourners left.

The men whose job it was to fill the grave with earth looked at the expensive car and the man inside. Then one of them said, "man, that's *living!*"

Unexpected Reunion

A story by Johann Peter Hebel* (adapted for ESL).

"Well, my love," called the young miner to his pretty fiancée one morning as he passed her window on his way to the mine, "on St. Lucy's Day our love will be blessed by the hand of the pastor, and we will be husband and wife!"

"How wonderful!" she called back to him, throwing him a kiss. "And ⁵ will we then build the little nest of our own which we have been planning?"

"Of course we will!" he said, raising his hand toward her. "And it will be a place of peace and love."

"It sounds too good to be true!" she said clasping her hands together ¹⁰ in a feeling of joy.

"But it *will* be true!" he answered confidently. "What can keep our dream from coming true?"

She leaned out of the window so that she could speak more softly as she said with a note of seriousness in her voice, "As for me, I would ¹⁵ rather be in my grave than live without you, for you are *everything* to me!"

"And you to me!" he replied with a broad smile. Then he left for his daily work underground, turning around several times on his way to wave to his love before she disappeared in the distance behind him in ²⁰ the predawn light of morning.

---

*Johann Peter Hebel (1760–1826) lived and wrote in Germany. He became a priest and served as a teacher and school principal. Later in life he was made a bishop.

The Sunday before St. Lucy's day they sat together in the church with their parents on either side of them. He held her hand tightly as they heard the pastor call out, "Does anyone know any reason why Swen Olson and Anna Larson should not be joined in marriage? If not, they shall be married in the Lord's house next week." There were no words on the lips of the people in the congregation—only nods of approval and smiles. Swen and Anna smiled, too, as they glanced at each other shyly.

Death, however, gave an answer to the pastor's question the next day. For though the young man stopped below the window of his beloved to bid her "Good morning!" as he always did, he never returned to wish her "Good night." Little did his beloved Anna know that the black miner's clothes that she saw him wear that morning would be his death garb. He went to the pit underground that day, after waving to her happily, whistling as he went, but was killed in a cave-in before the end of the day.

It so happened that the day her beloved Swen was buried in the mine, the young bride-to-be had sewed a black kerchief with a red border for him to wear with his wedding suit. When they told her that he was interred deep in the earth and was never found by his fellow workers, she laid aside the kerchief and wept for him. And because she could not forget him, she decided not to marry another.

This happened in a little village in Sweden in the year 1759. Then, fifty years passed.

During those fifty years, history was made: Wars were begun in animosity and ended in peace; some countries, including America, gained their independence, and others had their borders changed. Also, kings and queens were born, and some died.

Fifty years passed, during which there were times of good harvests and times of natural disasters.

Fifty years passed, during which, also, the peasants sowed and reaped, the millers ground, the smithies hammered, and the miners kept digging for ore in their workshops underground.

In 1809, in the month of June, somewhere around St. John's Day, the miners in this little village in Sweden were making an opening between two shafts at least six hundred feet below the earth. As they dug in the rocky earth and vitriol water, to their great surprise, they found the corpse of a young man. The body was completely permeated with iron sulfate, but other than that, it was unimpaired and unchanged. In fact, the men who found him could fully recognize the features of his face and estimate his age. It was almost as if he had died no more than an hour before or had fallen asleep on his job.

The body was brought to the surface, but none of the miners recognized him or knew, after all these years, of the tragedy which had claimed the life of the young man. In the hope of finding someone who might know him, they asked everyone in the district, including the women, to come and view the body. One by one they all passed by to look, but no one was able to identify the young man.

Then a little old lady, grey and shriveled, walked by on crutches, viewing with the rest. It was Anna Larson, who was seventy years old. She came only because *all* had been asked. With her eyes, dim with age, she glanced at the youth. Then, as she looked more closely, her heart almost stopped, for she saw that it was her beloved Swen.

She bent down over him and wept, more in happiness than in sadness, at the thought of seeing him again.

When Anna recovered from her burst of emotions, she said to the others standing there, "It is my fiancé, Swen Olson, to whom I was promised fifty years ago! Less than a week before we were to be married, he went down into the earth and never returned! Now God has allowed me to see him again before I die."

The hearts of all those who were there with her were overcome with sorrow, and they wept as they observed the still-preserved, handsome features of the young man in contrast with the withered figure of the elderly woman. It was too much for some of them to see the elderly woman so full of emotion beside the silent corpse of the young man whose lips were unable to give a little smile or utter a word, and whose eyes were unable to indicate recognition.

The next day, when the grave was made ready for him in the churchyard, the people of the village and all the miners came to bid him farewell. Anna stood in front of all the others, next to the young pastor who read the burial service. Then, before the body was lowered, Anna unlocked a little box which she carried and took out the black kerchief with the red border which she had made for him to wear at their wedding. She bent over his body and tied the kerchief neatly on the neck of her lifeless groom.

Then, as she stood there in her Sunday best, dressed more for a wedding than a funeral, she spoke in a firm voice: "Sleep well now, and may the time not be long before I join you. I have only a few more things to take care of, and then you can be sure that I will come to lie beside you." She took a deep breath as though to compose herself. Then she looked around at the many people there, most younger than she, and saw that there was not a dry eye on any of the faces. She, however, was not weeping; she had wept her last.

She looked down again at the body of her beloved Swen and con-
105   tinued, "And soon, then, will come the resurrection, the second one for
you and the best. What the earth has relinquished to be with *us* briefly,
it will not refuse to give up a second time to be with *God* eternally!"
After bowing her head in silent prayer, she turned and walked slowly
away. Then she looked back once more and saw men, with rough
110   miner's hands, weep as they lowered into the earth the body of a person
none of them had known.

A.   Questions on the content of the story.
Mark *T* for *true* and *F* for *false*. Be ready to give a reason for your
answer.

_____   **1.** As the story begins, the two young people are speaking with each other in Anna's house.

_____   **2.** Swen asked Anna to marry him one morning before
he left for the mine.

_____   **3.** Their plan was to live with Anna's family after they
were married.

_____   **4.** Anna and Swen appeared to love each other very
much.

_____   **5.** The Sunday before they were to be married they attended church together.

_____   **6.** The day Swen died he again stopped to say "Good
morning" to Anna.

_____   **7.** The day he died Swen wore black clothes in the mine.

_____   **8.** Swen seemed to know that he was going to die.

_____   **9.** Anna sewed the black kerchief for Swen because she
thought he was going to die.

_____   **10.** When Swen died in the mine, his fellow workers
knew where he was but decided not to take his body
out.

_____   **11.** Swen Olson died in the eighteenth century.

_____   **12.** Fifty years later was shortly after the beginning of the
nineteenth century.

_____ 13. During those fifty years, the United States of America became an independent nation.

_____ 14. Anna had a very unhappy marriage to another man during a part of those fifty years.

_____ 15. Swen's body was found in the mine in winter.

_____ 16. Swen looked the same when they found him as when he died.

_____ 17. The miners who found his body did not know who Swen was.

_____ 18. The miners asked everyone in the district to go into the underground mine to view the body.

_____ 19. Anna looked very different than she had looked fifty years before.

_____ 20. When Anna recognized her beloved Swen, she could not look at him.

_____ 21. Anna told the people who Swen was.

_____ 22. Anna was happy that God had let her see Swen once more.

_____ 23. Swen Olson was buried in a grave one day after Anna saw and recognized him.

_____ 24. The same pastor who was going to marry them fifty years before read the burial service for Swen.

_____ 25. Anna spoke at the burial service.

_____ 26. She wept as she spoke, but the other people did not.

_____ 27. Swen's body was lowered into the grave by miners who had worked with him underground.

B. Vocabulary practice.

1. Underline the best answer.
   a. A *fiancée* is a woman who is (engaged to be married/ already married/a bride), and a *fiancé* is a (man/miner/ pastor) who is engaged to be married.
   b. *Predawn* light is light (after daybreak/at daybreak/before daybreak).

    c. The people of the congregation gave *nods of approval* for Swen and Anna in the church, which means that they thought (Swen and Anna should be married/Swen and Anna shouldn't be married/one of them would die).

    d. Death *garb* refers to (a coffin/clothes/a grave).

    e. To *inter* means to (find/bury/die).

    f. To *weep* means to (cry/feel sad/have tears in the eyes).

    g. *Animosity* means more or less the same as (hostility/anxiety/animation).

    h. To *sow* means to (plow/work/plant).

    i. To *reap* means to (harvest/work/tear).

    j. To *permeate* means more or less the same as (destroy/penetrate/make permanent).

    k. To *impair* means more or less the same as (repair/injure/prepare).

    l. When it says that the miners did not know of the *tragedy* which took Swen's life, it means that they didn't know about the (disastrous event/vitriol water/mine shaft) which killed him.

    m. *Shriveled* means more or less the same as (old/sick/wrinkled).

    n. When it says that Anna was *withered*, it means that she was (wrinkled/sick/on crutches).

    o. *Resurrection* means the act of (rising into the air/rising from the dead/being with God eternally).

2. Match the *opposites*.

a. build	**1.** remember
b. leave	**2.** tear down
c. appear	**3.** join
d. forget	**4.** lower
e. find	**5.** lose
f. raise	**6.** disappear
	7. return

3. Work with homonyms.

Homonyms are words with the same pronunciation but with different spelling.

Examples: there   their
            here   hear

Find homonyms *in this story* for these words.

     a. sew _____

     b. minor _____

     c. past _____

     d. piece _____

     e. new _____

     f. weak _____

     g. or _____

     h. aloud _____

     i. red _____

C. Grammar practice.

Write the correct form of the verb (look for indications of tense, for example, in the sentences).

1. Anna and Swen had _____ to build a house
   (plan)
   of their own.

2. When she heard him speak of their marriage, she

   _____ it sounded too good to be true.
   (think)

3. When I saw her, she was _____ out of the
   (lean)
   window to talk to him.

4. Have you ever _____ out of a window like
   (lean)
   that?

5. Had he ever _____ to her like that before?
   (speak)

6. When the pastor asked the question in church, Anna and Swen

   were _____ with their parents.
   (sit)

7. I think the pastor had _____ that question
   (ask)
   at least once before.

8. He _____ the same day that she sewed
   (die)

   the kerchief.

9. When she hears his name, she _____ for
   (weep)

   him.

10. Swen always whistled as he _____ to work.
    (walk)

11. The miners had not _____ in that place for
    (dig)

    a long time.

12. The miners _____ the body to the surface.
    (bring)

13. No one _____ Swen until Anna came along.
    (recognize)

14. They thought maybe he _____ asleep.
    (fall)

15. None of the miners had ever _____ him
    (see)

    before.

16. Did she _____ him the day he died?
    (see)

17. After she recognized him, they _____
    (make)

    ready his grave.

18. When the pastor finished the service, Anna _____
    (speak)

    to Swen.

19. Hadn't any of the miners _____ him?
    (know)

20. The men were _____ when they lowered
    (weep)

    his body into the grave.

D. Questions for discussion.

1. What do you think is meant by *being blessed by the hand of the pastor?*

2. Do you think Anna and Swen were religious people? Explain.

3. Why do you suppose they sat with their parents in church?

4. The custom at that time was to ask in the church at least twice before the wedding if anyone objected to the marriage. Is there a similar custom in your country? Explain.

5. What do you think Anna and Swen meant by a *nest* of their own?

6. Do you think Anna made the right decision when she decided not to marry another man? Explain.

7. What do you think of the way the author illustrated the passing of fifty years? Explain.

8. Do you think it is possible for a body to be preserved in this way so that it could be recognized after fifty years? Explain.

9. What do you think was the main reason the people wept at Swen's burial?

E. Writing practice (or more discussion).

1. Write a paragraph describing (or describe to the class) Anna, Swen, or both.

2. Write a paragraph (or tell the class) about the feelings you had when you heard or read this story? Include what you think was a *reason* for your feelings.

3. Write a paragraph (or tell the class) about a mine tragedy which you know of from your country.

4. Write a paragraph (or speak to the class) about someone you know, or have heard of, who spoke at the funeral or burial of a loved one. Include your opinion about whether you thought it was a good idea or not.

5. Write a paragraph (or tell the class) about someone you know, or have heard of, who did not marry after being hurt or grieved over losing the one he or she was going to marry.

F. Food for thought.

An Unexpected Answer

Since this story took place in Sweden and is about a religious person, it reminds me of a Swedish farmer I worked for in Minnesota, whom I'll call Knut.

Knut was a religious man and a hard worker. His land was not the greatest, but a tenth of whatever it produced was given to the Lord, and he never missed church on Sunday.

One day, a neighbor of his leaned over a fence near where Knut was working and said, "Knut, I always see you work so hard here, and I know that you give a lot to the church. Now, you know I don't think much of this religion business, so I tried something."

"What was that?" asked Knut, as he paused to listen to his neighbor.

"Well, you see this field here?" he said gesturing. "I worked the land *on Sunday*, I sowed it *on Sunday*, and I harvested it *on Sunday*. And do you know what?" he said with a broad smile. "It produced better than ever before."

Knut took his straw hat off, wiped his brow, and said with a friendly smile, "There's one thing, Jessy, that you have to remember."

"What's that?"

"Well, the Lord doesn't always settle all of his accounts in September."

Marta

Based on an incident told by a student from Norway.

"Maybe we should look for a place to stay in this next village," my husband, Lars, said, as he slowed the car to a crawl. "It's only five o'clock, but it's too dark for driving steep, winding roads which I've never seen before."

5   "It's fine with me," I replied from the seat beside him. "Let's see if they have one of those little hotels right on the fjord. Maybe it will turn out to be one of those places where you can learn some history that's not in the history books."

    My husband laughed as he maneuvered the car around a hairpin turn
10 and down a very steep hill into the village. He had been recently appointed chairman of the department of history at the university where he had been teaching for almost twenty years. He loved teaching history, and he almost equally loved his favorite hobby, which was visiting out-of-the-way places where "history" is passed on by word of mouth
15 from one generation to the other. At the moment, we were on our way to see some old friends who had moved to a coastal town in southern Norway. We had taken a back road in hopes of finding a quaint village along the way which we had never visited.

    As Lars drove slowly down the main street of the village, he saw a
20 sign that said GUEST HOUSE. "This looks like a good place, Lily," he said with a smile as he looked toward me. "What do you want to bet we'll meet some interesting people here?"

    "I think you're right," I answered, "and we'll probably be their only guests."

190

As we walked into the lobby of the small hotel, a little, old man with   25
gray hair and a beard greeted us as he looked over the top of his reading
glasses. He puffed on a small pipe as he checked us in.

"Is it always so peaceful here?" I asked as I looked out of a window
overlooking the fjord and the nearby mountains.

"Yup, it sure is," the old man answered as he nodded. "We don't   30
allow anything but peace here," he added with an impish smile. Then
he got up out of his squeaky chair, stroked his beard, and said, "I can't
think of anything that could upset anybody here, unless he'd bring it in
from someplace else."

We all smiled as my husband said, "Sounds good to us; we want a   35
peaceful night's sleep."

"Can't see why you wouldn't get it here," the old man said, as he
started to lead the way toward our room, "unless, like I said, you
brought something with you to keep you awake."

"My name is Swenson," he said, as he showed us the room. "This old   40
house has been in my family since it was built in 1852, 103 years ago."

"I'll bet it has an interesting history," Lars commented, looking
around.

"Well, there's not too much out of the ordinary here. We Swensons
have always been just plain folks." Then he looked around the room he   45
had led us into and said, "This was my grandmother's room."

I noticed that everything had the appearance of being from the last
century. "The room looks very special, Mr. Swenson," I said, touching
the dark, shiny wood on the beautiful four-poster bed in the middle of
the room. "Are you sure you want us to stay here?"   50

"Yes, I'm sure," he said in a definite voice, as though he were wondering what was wrong with me to ask a question like that. "Gramma
would be glad to have you use her room."

"Oh, I didn't mean it that way," I added apologetically.

He smiled. Then he continued, "By the way, there are no locks on   55
any of these doors. I hope that won't upset you." When we assured him
that it wouldn't, he invited us to have dinner with him in the kitchen.

After a good fish dinner and an interesting talk with "Grampa" Swenson, as he asked us to call him, we retired to our room. The warmth
from the fireplace felt good as we got ready for bed.   60

Although it was only eight o'clock, it was unbelievably quiet in the
village. It seemed as though all of the people had gone to bed at the
same time. The only sound we could hear was from a dog which appeared to be carrying on a conversation with a canine friend somewhere
up on the hill.   65

    I sat by the window for a moment, from where I could see the few of the lights in the streets of the village which were still on. The water of the fjord below looked like glass as the moon shone upon it, and the snow on the roofs, reflected in the moonlight, looked like warm, white
70 blankets for the families under them. It truly seemed to be what Grampa Swenson said: Nothing could upset you here. I certainly was sitting in the most peaceful place in the world. Wanting to say something to Lars, I turned around but saw that he was already asleep.

    After thirty-five years of marriage I had learned that he needed these
75 times away from the pressures of the university. It was good to see him sleep so peacefully. I turned out the light and got into bed. Instead of trying to sleep, however, I sat up in the bed and gazed into the embers in the fireplace. As the flicker of the fire made shadows dance on the wall, I became lost in thought.

80   Suddenly I was shaken out of my trance by the sound of a child crying. "How sound carries in such a quiet place!" I thought to myself. "It almost seems as though that child is in this room." Then I heard it again. This time it seemed to be only a few feet away from me.

    "Is someone there?" I said almost in a whisper, hoping not to awaken
85 Lars. No one answered, but then I heard the soft, plaintive crying again. I strained my eyes to see in the direction from which the sound seemed to be coming. Then I saw in the semidarkness the figure of a child. It seemed to be a girl, perhaps about seven or eight, dressed in a nightgown of an old style.

90   "Momma?" the child said softly. "My momma?" Somehow the speech seemed to be that of a much younger child than she appeared to be.

    "Have you lost your way, little girl?" I said, trying to speak as kindly as possible. I thought maybe she had wandered in from another room,
95 although I didn't see any other guests.

    At the sound of my voice, the child seemed to draw back. I decided to switch on a table lamp nearby to get a better look. When I got up from the chair, the child drew back into the corner of the room.

    I turned on the light and looked. There was *no one* there! "What is
100 this?" I said aloud to myself. Then I looked all around the room, even under the bed. I opened the door and looked down the hallway but saw *nothing, anywhere*! Chills ran up and down my spine at the thought of having seen something more out of the ordinary than I thought I would at a place like this.

105   Needless to say, I didn't sleep much. I spent most of the night sitting in front of the fire with the light off, hoping to see the child again, but I didn't.

I wondered, finally, toward morning whether I really had seen and heard anything at all. After all, I was lost in thought. But it seemed so real! I sat for a long time in silence, the only sound still being the dogs outside, which hadn't finished their discussion.

Finally, Lars woke up, and I told him what I had seen and heard. He didn't know what to make of it either. As soon as we heard someone stir in the kitchen, we dressed and went down. Grampa Swenson was there, pouring a cup of coffee, while a cook was making breakfast. He asked us to have breakfast with him, so we sat down.

I wanted to tell Grampa Swenson what I had seen and heard, but I didn't quite know how to start. Finally, I made an attempt. "We—I think—that is—we had a little visitor in our room last night."

"You did?" he said. "Well, I'll have to set a trap tonight or get the cat in there. I'm sorry about that."

"It wasn't a mouse, Grampa Swenson," I said, getting up my courage. "It was a little girl about seven or eight years old, who spoke like a much younger child. And she seemed to disappear when I turned on the light."

Grampa Swenson leaned forward, closed one eye, took his pipe out of his mouth, and said, "That's Marta! By golly, I believe you saw Marta! Funny thing, she hasn't come now for a number of years."

"Who's Marta?" I asked, feeling somewhat relieved to think that maybe I hadn't seen things, after all.

"Marta," Grampa Swenson began, as he sat back again and puffed a little on his pipe, "was my father's little sister. She was born shortly after this house was built. She had a very high fever when she was about two and was never right in her mind after that. When she was about eight or nine, her mother died. I guess that poor little girl was so attached to her mother, she couldn't live without her. Not six months after her mother died, Marta passed away, too."

We both sat there not knowing what to say. Then Lars said, "Are you telling us, Grampa Swenson, that this Marta, who died nearly a century ago, has appeared here a number of times since her death?"

"Yup, that's what I'm telling you. A number of people have seen her over the years, and I saw her once myself, about ten years ago. She comes back. I don't know why, but she does."

We still didn't know what to say. Grampa Swenson was speaking about this as though it were something as ordinary as the sunshine—like something which should bother no one.

"By golly, it's the first of November today, isn't it?" asked Grampa Swenson looking over his glasses.

"Yes, it is," I replied, glancing at the calendar on the kitchen wall.

150   "That figures," said Grampa Swenson, stroking his beard and raising his eyebrows. "She always comes the night before All Saints' Day. That's the night she died, you see. It was in 1860, I think."

    Grampa Swenson saw the puzzled looks on our faces. Then, with a deep chuckle he said, "It didn't scare you, did it, to have Marta come to
155 see you?"

    Again, we didn't know quite what to say.

    "I sure hope something like that won't keep nice folks like you from coming back to see us again."

    We looked at each other. Then Lars said, "No, I suppose it won't
160 keep us from returning, but if it's all the same to you, we may try to make sure we don't come the night before All Saints' Day." Then, smiling broadly, he added, "That way nothing will bother us except what we bring along."

    Grampa Swenson smiled, tapped his finger in his pipe, and reached
165 for the tobacco pouch in his back pocket. Then, out of the corner of his one open eye, he looked at us and said, "Well, if this kind of thing *does* bother you, it may be better if you didn't come New Year's Eve either. You might meet Sonja."

    We looked at each other again, not knowing if we should ask who
170 Sonja was. But we were both pretty sure that if we did, we'd learn a little more history that isn't found in history books.

A.   A true-or-false quiz on the content of the story.

    Mark *T* for *true* and *F* for *false*. Be ready to give a reason in class for your answer.

    _____   **1.** As the story begins, Lars and Lily are in a car.

    _____   **2.** The story takes place in the mountains of Norway.

    _____   **3.** Lars taught the history of small towns.

    _____   **4.** Lars and Lily did not want to stay at a large hotel.

    _____   **5.** They had stayed in this village many times.

    _____   **6.** A man checked them into the guest house.

    _____   **7.** It was very quiet in this village.

    _____   **8.** The guest house was built in the nineteenth century.

    _____   **9.** Grampa Swenson told them they could stay in Marta's room.

_____ 10. Lars and Lily locked their door before they went to bed.

_____ 11. Lily heard some dogs barking.

_____ 12. There was no snow in the village when Lars and Lily arrived.

_____ 13. Lars and Lily had been married more than twenty-five years at this time.

_____ 14. Lily went to sleep before her husband did.

_____ 15. Lars saw the little girl before Lily did.

_____ 16. The little girl that appeared in Lars and Lily's room seemed to be very bright.

_____ 17. Lily looked under the bed and out of the door because she was afraid.

_____ 18. Lily did not tell Lars about the girl until he woke up in the morning.

_____ 19. Lily had a hard time finding the words to tell Grampa Swenson about the girl.

_____ 20. When Lily said they had had a *little visitor* in the room, Grampa Swenson thought they meant that they had seen a mouse.

_____ 21. When Lily described the girl, Grampa Swenson could not think of who it was.

_____ 22. Grampa Swenson told them that Marta and her mother had died on the same day.

_____ 23. Lars and Lily arrived the last day of one month and stayed until the first day of the next.

_____ 24. When Marta appeared, it was always on the anniversary of her death.

_____ 25. Grampa Swenson hoped that Lars and Lily would come back to visit them again.

_____ 26. Grampa Swenson told them to come back so they could meet Sonja.

B. Vocabulary practice.

    1. Underline the best answer.

      a. Lars slowed the car to a *crawl*, which means that (he drove very slowly/they went on their hands and knees/the hills were steep).

      b. *Winding* roads have many (straight sections/steep hills/ curves).

      c. A *fjord* has (salt water/fresh water/no water).

      d. Lars *maneuvered* the car on the mountain road, which tells you that he was probably driving (carelessly/ carefully/with ease).

      e. A *hairpin turn* on a mountain road is one with a (sharp curve/steep hill/narrow roadway).

      f. A *back* road is usually traveled (a lot/little/not at all).

      g. A *guest house* is usually a (small/large/old) place to stay.

      h. To *allow* means to (speak loud/let/stay).

      i. There are *embers* in a (fire/shadow/fireplace).

      j. To *get ready* means more or less the same as to (compare/ impair/prepare).

      k. A *four-poster* bed is one with (a post on each corner/four posts on each side/a canopy).

      l. When Grampa Swenson said that nothing could *upset* them, he meant that nothing could (hurt/scare/bother) them.

      m. When Lily said that she was *in a trance*, she meant that she was (lost in thought/sleepy/asleep).

      n. *Plaintive* crying is like crying out of (anger/ happiness/suffering).

      o. *Semidarkness* means (partial darkness/total darkness/ flickering light).

      p. To *wonder* means to (wander/wish to know something/ doubt).

      q. They heard someone *stir* in the kitchen, which means that they heard someone (move about/mix something/cook breakfast).

      r. When Grampa Swenson said, "*Funny thing*, she hasn't come now for a number of years," he meant that it was (laughable/serious/strange) that she hadn't come.

      s. When he said that Marta was *not right in her mind*, he meant that she was (not mentally normal/never correct about anything/attached to her mother).

    t. To *come back* means about the same as to (return/appear/visit).

    u. *Pass away* is an expression meaning (leave/disappear/die).

    v. A *chuckle* is a little (puff/laugh/shout).

  2. Match the *opposites.*

a. return	**1.** disallow
b. teach	**2.** leave
c. let	**3.** wander
d. cry	**4.** lower
e. lose	**5.** find
f. raise	**6.** learn
	7. laugh

C. Grammar practice.

  1. Practice with prepositions.

    Write *in, on,* or *at* in each of the blanks.

    a. They were driving _____ a mountain road.

    b. Lars and Lily decided to stay _____ a little village.

    c. They stopped driving _____ five o'clock.

    d. Grampa Swenson was _____ the lobby of the guest house when they arrived.

    e. The moonlight reflected _____ the fjord.

    f. A fjord has sea water _____ it.

    g. Not all history is _____ books.

    h. She looked _____ the mountains.

    i. I think there was tobacco _____ his pipe.

    j. He put the pipe _____ top of the table.

    k. "I think there is someone _____ the door," she said.

    l. There seemed to be someone else _____ the room.

    m. Lars was _____ bed, sleeping.

    n. They live _____ the city.

o. They live ＿＿＿＿＿＿ Tenth Street.

p. They live ＿＿＿＿＿＿ 213 Tenth Street.

q. Are you sure they are supposed to stay ＿＿＿＿＿＿ this room?

r. He was dressed ＿＿＿＿＿＿ a new suit.

s. He had ＿＿＿＿＿＿ a new suit.

t. The cup was ＿＿＿＿＿＿ the table.

u. The coffee was ＿＿＿＿＿＿ the cup.

v. He always had breakfast ＿＿＿＿＿＿ six o'clock.

2. Write the correct form of the verb.

a. He had never ＿＿＿＿＿＿＿＿ on this road be-
(drive)
fore.

b. When they had time, they ＿＿＿＿＿＿＿
(visit)
small villages.

c. She didn't ＿＿＿＿＿＿＿ with him.
(speak)

d. In fact, she has never ＿＿＿＿＿＿＿ with him.
(speak)

e. Did he always ＿＿＿＿＿＿＿ them in a friend-
(greet)
ly way?

f. He said they didn't ＿＿＿＿＿＿＿ anything
(allow)
but peace there.

g. He did not ＿＿＿＿＿＿＿ up at first.
(get)

h. He had not ＿＿＿＿＿＿＿ up in a long time.
(get)

i. Everyone had ＿＿＿＿＿＿＿ to bed by eight
(go)
o'clock.

   j. Something _____ her out of her trance.
                (shake)

   k. The girl was _____ in a nightgown of
                (dress)
   an old style.

   l. By the time she turned on the light, the child had

   _____.
   (disappear)

   m. When Lars is at peace, he _____ well.
                (sleep)

   n. Marta had been _____ a number of
                (see)
   times before.

D. Questions for discussion.

   1. Do you think it is unusual for a teacher of history to be interested in the type of history that is not in books? Explain.

   2. Do you think staying in a small hotel is usually more interesting than staying in a large one? Explain.

   3. Do you think Lars and Lily *hoped* they would be the only guests in this guest house? Explain.

   4. Do you think the people in small towns have fewer problems than people in large cities? Explain.

   5. Lily tells this story. Do you think it would be different if Lars were telling it? Explain.

   6. Lily did not seem to be frightened by what she saw. Why do you suppose she wasn't?

   7. What do you think you would have done if you had seen and heard what Lily did?

   8. Why do you suppose that Lily later had some doubt about whether she had actually seen or heard the little girl?

   9. Do you think Lily thought that maybe Grampa Swenson would know something about the little girl? Explain.

   10. Why do you suppose Grampa Swenson didn't seem to be bothered by the appearance of Marta?

   11. The day before All Saints' Day is Halloween. Do you think this had anything to do with Marta's appearance? Explain.

E. Writing practice (or more discussion).

1. Write a paragraph (or tell the class) about what kind of relationship you think Lars and Lily had.
2. Write a paragraph explaining (or explain to the class) an unusual experience you have had.
3. Write a paragraph (or tell the class) about an interesting out-of-the-way place you have visited.
4. Write a paragraph (or tell the class) about a retarded person you knew, or heard of, who died soon after the death of a person to whom he or she was very attached.
5. Look up *Halloween* and *All Saints' Day*. Write a paragraph (or tell the class) about their origin and meaning.

F. A bit of humor.

Father (to ten-year-old son): What did you learn in school today?
Son: I learned how to say "yes, sir" and "no, sir."
Father: You did?
Son: Yup.

A man who did not believe in going to church pulled up to a gas station in a small town in the State of Maine. As the station attendant, a local man of about sixty, was filling the gas tank, the man said to him, gesturing with his hand, "Look at that—two churches across the street from each other. They say they're going to the same place, so why do they need different churches?"

The local man replied with gestures of his own, "I don't think you understand, mister. That church over there says, 'there is no hell,' and that one over there says, 'the hell there isn't!'"

The Open Window

A Story by Saki (H. H. Munro), adapted for ESL.

"My aunt will be down in a minute, Mr. Nuttel," said the girl who had let him in a few minutes earlier. "In the meantime, you will have to put up with me. I'm Mrs. Sappleton's niece."

Framton Nuttel listened nervously to the girl and answered her ques-
5 tions the best he could. He couldn't imagine how a girl of fifteen could speak to a stranger so boldly and act with such poise. He, at fifty-five, was not half that confident. And he remembered that at fifteen, he hardly spoke to anyone.

"Do you know many of the people around here?" asked the niece.
10 "Hardly a soul," he said, looking toward the stairway, where he hoped Mrs. Sappleton would appear soon. "My sister lived here during the summer a few years ago. She liked it very much. When she knew I was coming to stay here for awhile, she gave me some letters of intro-duction to some of the people in the community."

15 Framton wondered now whether he should have promised his sister that he'd meet these people. He felt so uneasy about it. But he remem-bered how his sister pleaded, "Framton, please meet some of the lovely people there! It will do you good! It will do you no good at all to go to a rural retreat for a nerve cure if you just sit there in the cottage."

20 "So, then," the girl went on, "you know almost nothing about my aunt?"

"Only her name and address. I have never met her," admitted the caller. He was even wondering whether Mrs. Sappleton was, perhaps, a widow. Somehow the room suggested that there was a man living there, too. But he thought little more about it.   25

"Then you know nothing of my aunt's tragedy, Mr. Nuttel?" asked the girl, lowering her voice.

"Tragedy? No, my sister didn't mention anything about a tragedy."

"When was your sister here last?"

"Four or five years ago."   30

"Well," she continued just above a whisper, "this happened three years ago. In fact, it was three years ago today."

To a man like Framton Nuttel, it seemed like all tragedies occurred in big cities. Somehow big problems seemed out of place in this restful country spot. But he listened to the girl as she went on in a soft voice.   35
"You may wonder why we keep that window open on an October afternoon," she said, pointing to a large French window that opened to the lawn.

"It is quite warm for this time of the year," said Framton; "but, does the window have something to do with the tragedy?"   40

"Yes, it does," she went on, still speaking just above a whisper. "Out of that window, three years ago today, my aunt's husband and her two younger brothers went for a day's shooting. They never came back."

Framton listened with interest at the building mystery as the girl went on, leaning toward him in her chair. "They were crossing a foot-   45
bridge over a rushing stream. It broke while all three of them were on it." Her voice seemed to crack a little with emotion as she continued. "They never had a chance in a torrent like that. A rescue team went out later. But they never even recovered the bodies. The mouth of that stream is not too far from the open ocean. In a short time the men must   50
have washed out to sea. Poor things!"

The girl put her head into her hands. Then she raised her head again. Noticing that her listener had tears in his eyes, she sat up and seemed to regain her poise. "My poor dear aunt!" she said as she looked toward the stairs. "She thinks that someday, probably on an anniversary of their   55
death—like today—they will return. I have heard her say many times that she is sure that her husband, her two brothers, and the brown spaniel that was lost with them will return through that window—the way they went out."

Framton Nuttel didn't know what to think. And, certainly, he didn't   60
know what to say. The young girl noticed that the guest was getting more nervous by the minute. She looked around. Seeing that her aunt still was not coming down the stairs, she continued in a soft voice:

"What's more—my aunt thinks that when her husband returns through
that window, he will have his waterproof coat over his arm. And she also
thinks that her younger brother will be singing 'Bertie, Why Do You
Bound?' like he always did to tease her because she didn't like that song.
She told me, too," she continued, pointing toward the yard outside the
open window, "that she thinks all three of them will come across the
lawn one day toward that window with their guns in their hands. And
she even thinks that the dog will be running on ahead of them. Can you
believe that, Mr. Nuttel? Maybe you can't. But I'll tell you something.
If you would hear my aunt talk about it, you'd get a feeling that it's really
going to happen. It gives me a creepy feeling to talk about it." She broke
off with a little shudder.

It was a relief when the aunt finally came down the stairs and apolo-
gized for being late.

"I hope Vera has been amusing you," she said, as the girl left the
room.

"Oh—oh, yes, she has," he replied.

Mrs. Sappleton looked toward the open window. "I hope you don't
mind the open window. I expect my husband and brothers anytime.
They've been out shooting and they always come in this way." Then she
talked with Framton, but she didn't give him full attention because she
looked so frequently toward the window.

"How strange!" he said to himself, "She obviously really does expect
the men to come!" Framton became so nervous he didn't know what to
do with himself. What an unfortunate coincidence—that he should
make this visit on the anniversary of this terrible tragedy! And the
woman had to make it worse by acting perfectly natural about expecting
the men to return—as though they had been gone only since the morning.

Finally, Mrs. Sappleton turned to Framton and gave him a moment's
attention: "And what brings you here to our rural community?" she
asked.

Imagining that it might be good for her to listen to someone else's
problems for a minute, he began, "My doctors ordered a complete rest
for me for at least three months without any mental excitement or
strenuous physical exercise." Since she actually seemed interested in
what he was telling her, he went on. "And, as for my diet, the doctors
said . . ."

"Here they are at last!" cried Mrs. Sappleton as she got up and went
toward the window. "Just in time for tea!"

Framton also got up. He couldn't believe his eyes! In the deepening

twilight he saw three figures and a dog walking across the lawn toward 105
the window! The men carried guns and one carried a raincoat over his
shoulder. They walked on silently. Then, as the dog started to run
toward the open window, one of the men broke into a chant of "Bertie,
Why Do You Bound?" Then they all three laughed.

Framton wildly grabbed his cane and his hat. He dashed out the door 110
and across the driveway to his car. Stones in the road went flying as he
sped away.

"Well, here we are, my dear," said the man who was carrying the
raincoat, as he came through the window. "But who was that who bolted
out as we came up?" 115

"A most extraordinary man—a Mr. Nuttel," said Mrs. Sappleton,
"who only could talk about his illness and dashed off without saying
good-bye when you arrived. One would think he had seen a ghost!"

"I think maybe it was the dog, auntie," said the girl, who had appeared again. "He told me he had a horror for dogs. In my conversation 120
with him, he told me how a pack of mad dogs chased him one time on
the banks of the Ganges River. He said he spent the night in a new
grave with the dogs snarling and foaming above him, and . . ."

Making up tall stories on short notice was the girl's specialty.

A. A true-or-false quiz on the content of the story.

Write *T* for *true* and *F* for *false*. Be ready, in class, to give a reason
for your answer.

_____ 1. Framton Nuttel had come to see Mrs. Sappleton, who
was an old friend of his.

_____ 2. Mrs. Sappleton told Mr. Nuttel that she didn't want
to talk to him.

_____ 3. Mrs. Sappleton's niece answered Mr. Nuttel's questions but said no more.

_____ 4. The girl was a teenager.

_____ 5. Framton Nuttel knew almost no one in that area.

_____ 6. Mr. Nuttel had come to this community on a business
trip.

_____ 7. Framton Nuttel's brother had suggested that he meet
people there.

_____ 8. The niece wanted to find out what Mr. Nuttel knew about her aunt, Mrs. Sappleton.

_____ 9. The girl said that Mrs. Sappleton's husband and brothers had died.

_____ 10. Mrs. Sappleton's niece knew approximately how and when the men would return.

_____ 11. The niece knew that a hunting dog would also return with them.

_____ 12. Vera stayed and listened to the conversation between her aunt and Mr. Nuttel.

_____ 13. The aunt knew nothing of what Vera had told Framton Nuttel.

_____ 14. Mr. Nuttel told Mrs. Sappleton why he had come to this area.

_____ 15. The ghosts of the men appeared in the window.

_____ 16. Framton Nuttel left the house when the men arrived.

_____ 17. Mr. Nuttel hurried out of the house because he felt that he should not be seen with Mrs. Sappleton.

_____ 18. Mrs. Sappelton's husband asked about Framton Nuttel.

_____ 19. Mrs. Sappleton knew the real reason Framton Nuttel left the house.

_____ 20. Vera also made up a story about why Mr. Nuttel might have left.

B. Vocabulary practice.

1. Underline the best answer.
   a. When Vera said her aunt would be *down* in a minute, she meant that she would (come down from upstairs/be sick in bed/lie down).
   b. *Poise* means more or less the same as (poison/ imagination/composure).
   c. When Mr. Nuttel said he knew *hardly a soul* in that area, he meant that he (knew everyone/knew no one/knew almost no one).

    d. To feel *uneasy* means to feel (apprehensive/fearful/sick).

    e. The *tragedy* this girl was speaking of was (a disastrous event/an event which was in the future/a happy event).

    f. A *French window* is (a large window which can be opened like a door/a window made in France/a window which has glass like in French cathedrals).

    g. What is called *shooting* in this story would be called (hunting/killing/hiking) in American English.

    h. A *rescue* team is two or more people who (go hunting/try to help people in trouble/look for people who have been killed).

    i. A *spaniel* is a type of (dog/gun/cat).

    j. A *creepy* feeling is one we might get when we have a (happy/sad/strange) experience.

    k. A *coincidence* is an occurrence of things happening at the same time (by someone planning them/by accident/by someone making a mistake).

    l. When Mrs. Sappleton said that Mr. Nuttel *dashed off*, she meant that he (left without saying goodbye/left in a hurry/left in anger).

    m. A *waterproof* coat is a coat you might wear when the weather is (cold/rainy/windy).

2. Match the *opposites.*

a. earlier	**1.** urban
b. rural	**2.** later
c. nervous	**3.** closed
d. soft	**4.** excited
e. open	**5.** loud
f. worse	**6.** calm
	7. better

C. Grammar practice.

  1. Write the correct form of the verb. (Look for indications of *tense.*)

    a. Framton Nuttel had _____ to this area
                          (come)
    to rest.

    b. The niece _____ him a tall story which
                     (tell)
    he believed.

c. When he was fifteen he didn't _____

(speak)

to people very easily.

d. He had not _____ many people in this

(meet)

community.

e. His sister had _____ him some letters

(give)

of introduction.

f. Do people in rural communities _____

(have)

problems, too?

g. The men had _____ out for the day.

(go)

h. Vera knew the men would come through the French win-

dow when she _____ Framton that

(tell)

story.

i. Does he _____ anything about these

(know)

people?

j. She said that the bodies of the men were never

_____.

(recover)

k. When she looked, she _____ that he

(see)

had tears in his eyes.

l. The window had not been _____.

(break)

m. When he looked the next time, he _____

(see)

Mrs. Sappleton coming down the stairs.

n. The men _____ in, just the way she

(come)

said they would.

    o. Have you ever _____ someone tell a

                           (hear)

   story like that?

  2. Choose the correct word to complete the sentence.

    a. She came in (lately/later) than I thought she would.
    b. He has a (horrible/horribly) fear of dogs.
    c. The girl spoke (bold/boldly).
    d. She was a very (confident/confidently) person.
    e. Mr. Nuttel was a (nervous/nervously) man.
    f. He even spoke (nervous/nervously).
    g. She told the story (interesting/interestingly).
    h. It was an (interesting/interestingly) story.
    i. She spoke quite (good/well) for a young girl.
    j. He spoke very (poor/poorly).
    k. He was a (poor/poorly) speaker.
    l. The one brother sang (joyful/joyfully) as he arrived.
    m. He was a (happy/happily) man.
    n. Mr. Nuttel left (quick/quickly).

D. Questions for discussion.

  1. Do you think Mr. Nuttel and his sister, who suggested he meet people in this community, were very different people? Explain.
  2. What do you think had happened to Framton Nuttel to have his doctor suggest a nerve cure?
  3. Why do you think this girl decided to tell Mr. Nuttel this tall story?
  4. When Vera saw that Mr. Nuttel was obviously believing every word she spoke, do you think she was encouraged to go on and tell more? Explain.
  5. Why do you think Vera looked frequently to see if her aunt was coming?
  6. Do you think Vera was a good storyteller? Explain.
  7. People think that telling *tall stories* is always *fun*. Can you think of a circumstance where it could be injurious or dangerous? Explain.
  8. Do you think Mr. Nuttel was the kind of person who liked to talk about himself? Explain.

E. Writing practice (or more discussion).

1. Write a paragraph describing (or speak to the class about) Mr. Nuttel. (Include what you think he did for a living, whether you think he was married or not, what kind of youth you think he had, and so on.)

2. Write a paragraph (or tell the class) about an experience you had which gave you a *creepy* feeling and/or made you *shudder*.

3. Imagine that you are Mr. Nuttel. Write a brief letter to your sister, telling her about your experience at the Sappletons' house. (Imagine that you have *not*, as yet, learned the truth about Mrs. Sappleton's husband and brothers).

4. Imagine you are Vera. Write an entry in your diary for the day Mr. Nuttel visited her aunt's house.

5. Write (or tell the class) about a *tall story* which you, or someone you know, told as true and was believed by someone.

F. A bit of humor.

Can you top these tall stories?

In part of the American Southwest, where rivers frequently dry up or slow to a trickle part of the year, there are sometimes very dangerous flashfloods, especially in the summer rainy season. But they say you can tell if a flashflood is coming because there is always a school of fish about a half mile ahead of it, kicking up the dust.

In Tombstone, Arizona, which they call today "The Town Too Tough to Die," they say there was a man, about a hundred years ago, who walked into the post office, saw a bulletin which read WANTED FOR MURDER, and asked if he could apply for the job.

Irregular Verbs

PRESENT INFINITIVE	PAST TENSE	PARTICIPLE
be (am, is, are)	was, were	been
bear	bore	born
beat	beat	beaten
become	became	become
begin	began	begun
bend	bent	bent
blow	blew	blown
break	broke	broken
bring	brought	brought
buy	bought	bought
burst	burst	burst
catch	caught	caught
choose	chose	chosen
come	came	come
cut	cut	cut
deal	dealt	dealt
dig	dug	dug
do	did	done
drink	drank	drunk
drive	drove	driven
eat	ate	eaten
fall	fell	fallen
feed	fed	fed
fight	fought	fought
find	found	found
forget	forgot	forgotten
forgive	forgave	forgiven
fly	flew	flown
freeze	froze	frozen
get	got	gotten (or got)
give	gave	given
go	went	gone
grow	grew	grown
hang*	hung	hung
have	had	had
hear	heard	heard
hide	hid	hidden (or hid)
hold	held	held
keep	kept	kept
know	knew	known
lay	laid	laid
lead	led	led
leave	left	left
let	let	let
lie	lay	lain

(continued)

*hang is used as a regular verb when it pertains to an act of execution or suicide (hang, hanged, hanged).

PRESENT INFINITIVE	PAST TENSE	PARTICIPLE
lose	lost	lost
make	made	made
mean	meant	meant
meet	met	met
pay	paid	paid
put	put	put
quit	quit	quit
read	read (pronounced *red*)	read
ride	rode	ridden
ring	rang	rung
rise	rose	risen
run	ran	run
say	said (pronounced *sed*)	said
see	saw	seen
seek	sought	sought
send	sent	sent
shake	shook	shaken
shed	shed	shed
shine*	shone	shone
show	showed	showed
sing	sang	sung
sit	sat	sit
sleep	slept	slept
slit	slit	slit
speak	spoke	spoken
spend	spent	spent
stand	stood	stood
steal	stole	stolen
swim	swam	swum
take	took	taken
teach	taught	taught
tell	told	told
think	thought	thought
throw	threw	thrown
understand	understood	understood
write	wrote	written
wake†	woke	woke
wear	wore	worn
weep	wept	wept
win	won	won

shine is also used as a regular verb, especially when it means *to apply a brilliant surface to something*, such as a car, shoes, or furniture.

†*wake* is also sometimes used as a regular verb (wake, waked, waked).